MW01283739

Recipes
from

Venice

First edition (Venice) published in 2014 by Hardie Grant Books.
This edition published in 2023 by Hardie Grant Books,
an imprint of Hardie Grant Publishing

Hardie Grant Books (London)
5th & 6th Floors
52-54 Southwark Street
London SE1 1UN

Hardie Grant Books (Melbourne)
Ground Floor, Building 1
658 Church Street
Melbourne, VIC 3121
www.hardiegrantbooks.com

English translations of *Libro per Cuoco* (*Book for Cook*) by Anonimo Veneziano
on pages 12, 46, 66, 154, 208, 221 and 223 © Louise Smithson
Venetian translations of Libro di cucina/ Libro per cuoco (14th/15th c.) by Anonimo
Veneziano, based on Ludovico Frati (ed.): Libro di cucina del secolo XIV. Livorno (1899),
Digital version (22.12.2000); v.1 on pages 12, 223 and 226 © Thomas Gloning.

All rights reserved. No part of this publication may be reproduced,
stored in a retrieval system or transmitted in any form by any means,
electronic, mechanical, photocopying, recording or otherwise,
without the prior written permission of the publishers and copyright holders.

The moral rights of the authors have been asserted.

Copyright text © Katie and Giancarlo Caldesi
Copyright photography © Helen Cathcart

British Library Cataloguing-in-Publication Data. A catalogue record
for this book is available from the British Library.

Recipes from Venice
ISBN: 978-1-78488-662-2
10 9 8 7 6 5 4 3 2 1
Publishing Director: Kajal Mistry
Acting Publishing Director: Emma Hopkin
Commissioning Editor: Kate Burkett
Senior Editor: Chelsea Edwards
Photographer: Helen Cathcart
Design + Illustration: A+B Studio (Amelia Leuzzi + Bonnie Eichelberger)
Proofreader: Vicky Orchard
Indexer: Cathy Heath
Production Controller: Martina Georgieva
Colour Reproduction by p2d
Printed and bound in China by Leo Paper Products Ltd.

MIX
Paper from
responsible sources
FSC
www.fsc.org
FSC™ C020056

Recipes from
Venice

Katie and Giancarlo Caldesi
Photography by Helen Cathcart

Hardie Grant
BOOKS

06 **Introduction**
17 **At the Bar**
59 **At the Bakery**
73 **At the Pasta Bar**
113 **Stocks, Rice, Beans and Soups**
151 **At the Rialto Market**
179 **At the Fish Market**
205 **At the Butchers**
225 **At the Patisserie**
264 **Katie and Giancarlo's Favourite Restaurants in Venice**
267 **Grazie, Thank You**
268 **Bibliography**
269 **Index**
272 **About the Authors**

Introduction

Giancarlo and I have been lost in Venice many times but we never care, because it is one of the most dazzlingly beautiful places in the world to lose yourself in. Each time we leave the city, aboard the waterbus to the airport, I have tears of sadness in my eyes. Giancarlo says that Venice is like a painting or a dream that never fades.

The more I write about food, the more I find myself writing about history. The two are inseparable and although the end result of my research will be a recipe that I can share, it will inevitably be bound up with the past. No more so than where Venice is concerned. The history of the dishes matches the history of the city.

In medieval and Renaissance times, Venice was one of the most prosperous cities in Europe. Situated on the Adriatic coast, it straddles East and West and so was able to dominate commerce in the Mediterranean, particularly the spice trade. Its doors were always open to the world, from crusaders and pilgrims to revellers and romantics drawn to the carnival atmosphere and the magical experience of floating on water past stunning palaces, villas and narrow alleyways amid

the ever-changing light. Nothing has changed in the architecture for centuries and Venetians hold onto their precious past as if with bared teeth, determined not to let it go.

But the subject of tourism has become a tough debate. As the island city's trading empire shrank along with its population (compare 190,000 in 1422 to the current count of only 55,000) Venice deliberately courted the tourist, and we know from our many restaurateur friends that tourism is vital for their businesses to survive. But there is another voice among locals that says Venice is in danger of losing its soul, when apartments lie empty because only Chinese and Russian visitors can afford them, yet inhabit them infrequently; and small butchers, bakers and food shops are being replaced by ever more shops selling glassware, masks and trinkets to visitors, made not locally, but in the Far East.

However, as one Venetian told me, 'the tourist searches; the traveller finds' and away from the obvious attractions there are food markets, family-run restaurants and *bacari* – traditional inns or bars serving *cicchetti* (the Italian version of tapas) – where you

can eat more cheaply and well. There is a list in the back of this book of some of the places that Giancarlo and I have visited, but there are many more if you take the time to find them.

Much of the food served in Venice is simple. Really simple. For example, very fresh fish and shellfish are cooked quickly and served with no more than a drizzle of delicious oil and a squeeze of lemon – although our friend Arianna says that you only serve fish with lemon if it is old; if it is fresh you serve it naked. I think she means the fish.

We love this simplicity, but what a dramatic contrast, we thought, to the exotic, sensual spice-filled cooking that was once served; when the more lavishly your dishes were filled with pepper, cloves, nutmeg and saffron, the better. Spices were bling. Whatever happened to those splendid dishes of the past, we wondered? And so Giancarlo and I covered miles and miles of Venice's tiny alleyways, eating, talking, sampling and researching, in order to get to the heart of true Venetian cooking, steeped in the spicy, eclectic past of this stunning city.

Venetian Recipes Lost...

A Glimpse of Venetian History through Food

If I could only time travel I would visit the Rialto market in medieval days to wonder at the spices and taste some of the intricately decorated cakes that were all the rage since the new sugar craze hit town. I might feast with a patrician family in a palazzo on the Grand Canal in the late 15th century; or I might drop by in the 18th century to drink a hot chocolate in Florian's café with Giacomo Casanova.

Sometimes sitting in a Venetian café after a glass of wine or two, I try to imagine the city through the eyes of a European traveller during the Renaissance, arriving after a rough night at sea, perhaps running the gauntlet of pirates. You had heard of an amazing city called Venice and here you are: there are people with dark skin, pale skin, black hair, blonde hair. In the raunchiest areas, scantily clad women are beckoning, elsewhere glamorous people are spilling out of the opera house or ballrooms, hiding behind elaborate masks. And then there is the food: rich, spicy, sexy, exciting. It is a riot of colour and free living, a total assault on the senses. Perhaps you are a wealthy young gentleman on the Grand Tour, tired of the sedate cities of Florence and Rome, and now you can finally let your hair down in Venice.

One of the many things I have always loved about Italian cooking is the 'this is the way it has always been done, so this is the way it should stay' mentality, which ensures that the accurate reproduction of a classic dish is heralded just as much as the invention of a new one. In Venice, however, the classics that you find on menus, such as the *Baccalà*

Mantecato (see pages 181–81) – a whipped-up blend of salt cod, garlic and oil – and *Fegato alla Veneziana* (see page 212) – sliced liver and slow-cooked onions – show no signs of the rich heritage of spices, which seems incredible for a city largely built on its trade. In Calle degli Spezieri (Spice Alley) we found the last spice trader in town, Antica Drogheria Mascari, which dates back to 1948. Well worth a visit for its conical mounds of spices, dried mushrooms, truffles and tea; but why, we wanted to know, did Venetian cooks abandon spices in the second half of the 16th century?

As we began to delve more deeply into the heritage of Venetian cooking, we came to the conclusion that the dishes lost their spicy splendour when the city began to decline as a trading sovereignty, following years of war and the devastation left by two outbreaks of plague. When news reached Venice in 1499 that the explorer Vasco da Gama and his Portuguese navigators had rounded the Cape of Good Hope and reached India, Venice's monopoly on the spice trade was broken, and several commercial banks on the Rialto failed within days as a result.

Following the fall of the Roman Empire in the 5th century, many mainland Italians who had felt protected by the Romans were now in fear of attack by barbarians, so they escaped to the islands in the lagoons where they hid away and just about managed an existence. At least there was fish to eat and salt to trade. It was meant to be a temporary solution until the people felt it was safe to return, but that never happened and the first rough mud houses they built would one day give way to stunning gothic palazzi.

The first settlers developed the island of Torcello, and then began to build on the island we now know as Venice. According to legend, the city of Venice was officially founded on Friday 25 March AD 42 at midday, by emigrants from Padua who laid the first stone at the Rialto, the commercial area. The famous Rialto Bridge, the only one over the Grand Canal until the 19th century, was initially formed by a chain of boats in 1172. In 1200–60 it became a bridge made of wood and finally of stone in 1591. It must have been incredible to walk around the Rialto market and see the goods from the Levant and the Byzantium. By 1494 the Venetian historian Marino Sanudo il Giovane wrote that '... here in this land no thing grew, and yet everything was here in abundance, because everything from every land and every part of the world that could be eaten was brought here.' He also commented that by the evening nothing was left in the markets but empty stalls. The merchants sold metals, dyes, silks, gems and salt, often in return for timber, but above all they sold spice.

The Lure of Spice

It is often thought that in ancient times spices were used to disguise the off-flavour of old meat, and though spices were thought to help preserve foods, certainly while meat was being cured (a coating of pepper helps to keep insects away), I don't believe this applies to Venice, since only the rich could afford spices and they would have been able to buy fresh meat.

From the 12th century, the wealthy had become almost obsessed with spices. Venetian merchants would sail at particular times of the year to meet camel caravans and trains of pack animals bringing these luxuries from Asia and the Levant. Once back in Venice they would be sold for at least double their price to the rest of Italy and abroad. Salt, used as a valuable preservative as well as a flavour enhancer, was also produced in Venice and traded. And after the cunning marriage of a young Venetian bride to the King of Cyprus in 1468, Venice got its hands on that island and its sugar. Yet another commodity to bring Venetian families riches beyond their dreams.

This combination of a monopoly on spices, the production of salt and the trade in sugar is all reflected in the dishes of the Middle Ages and the Renaissance, along with the use of vinegar or verjuice, produced from the juice of young grapes. Foods were spicy, but also sweet and sour.

Sacchetti Veneti were little pouches of mixed spices that were used to flavour cooking in a similar way to a bouquet garni. Favourite individual spices used included:

Pepper including ground white, cubeb, black and long pepper were used in meat, fish and soup. Black pepper was the first spice to arrive, or at least be written about, in 853, when it appears in a record by Bishop Orso of Olivolo. Pepper was incredibly expensive, but it also lasted years, and was often handed down through families as a form of currency. In today's Venetian restaurants, many varieties are still favoured – we saw pink, white, green and black peppercorns, and Sichuan and long pepper being used frequently.

Cinnamon and cassia bark exported from India and Sri Lanka were used in casseroles, soups, omelettes and fish dishes. They were also used in sweets such as macaroni with sugar as a rich dessert.

Ginger was used with fish and meat, and in sauces and soups, often combined with pepper. It was also used in aromatic wines and with fruit. Imported in root form, it would most probably have dried by the time it reached Venice and so could be finely chopped or ground and used as a powder.

Cloves originated in the Molucca islands (now part of Indonesia) and also came from Madagascar and Sri Lanka. They were very expensive and used on roasted meat and in stews.

Nutmeg from India was used by the Arabs for medicinal reasons, and found its way into drinks, soups and spice bags.

Saffron arrived mainly from Persia or Asia Minor, but was also grown in Italy. It was used for colour more than flavour, in fritters, pastry, salami, tripe, sauces and soups.

Coriander seed, sumac, aniseed and many more were also available.

While the rich had their profusion of spices, the poor made do with fresh herbs such as thyme, marjoram, bay leaves, savoury, wild fennel, mint, garlic, sage and parsley, which were grown in the campi, the small fields between the houses.

The Republic

The year 697 saw the election of first Doge (Duke) of Venice, Paolo Lucio Anafesto, and the setting up of the Republic, which was divided much like London into specialist areas such as Del Ferro for ironmongery, Fondamenta del Vin for wines and Riva del Olio where the oil traders unloaded their caskets.

Over the years Venice made much of its republican constitution calling itself the Most Serene Republic of Venice as a specific reference to the Venetian government and the state authorities. The appellation 'most serene' is in fact an indicator of sovereignty and the same formula has been used by other republics within Europe over the centuries. However, it is only Venice that was, and still is, referred to as 'La Serenissima'.

In 1172, under the Doge, the Great Council was formed of aristocratic families, who in turn set up the Council of Ten in 1310 to deal with the unrest following a revolt against the Doge. Intended originally as a temporary measure, the Ten became a permanent body and among its various duties it wrote the laws aimed at controlling dress, gambling and vice, and also feasting and banqueting. There was a spiritual argument that vanity and greed would invoke the anger of the Almighty in a city that believed itself to be chosen by God. Meat and fish were not supposed to appear at the same meal. Oysters were not permitted where there were more than 20 guests. There were rules on the numbers of pastries and fruits that could be served, and peacocks and pheasants were forbidden foods. But no practical supervision was possible, so the laws were largely ignored and Venice still feasted, partied and held regattas whenever possible. It seems the ruling Council of Ten largely turned a blind eye since, as they said, 'with a full mouth, you can't say no,' i.e. if the people were allowed to party, it was a way of forestalling any rebellion.

Crusades and Carnevale

During the Crusades the Venetians helped the crusaders and pilgrims to find safe passage to the Holy Land. During the Fourth Crusade in 1203, the Doge Enrico Dandolo, 90 years old and blind, persuaded the knights to capture the town of Constantinople and, in return, provided them with transport. Constantinople remained in Venetian hands for the next half century until it was taken by the Nicene emperor Michael VIII Palaiologos. The spoils of the Venetian occupation (including the famous four horses now inside the Basilica of San Marco with replicas on the façade of the church) still decorate Venice's houses and museums. Jews, Arabs, Persians, Turks, Egyptians and Greeks all arrived in Venice over the years, settling in their own areas of the city and bringing with them their favourite ingredients and dishes with which to enrich Venetian cooking.

Symbolic of the Venetian dominance of the seas was the Arsenale di Venezia, Venice's complex of shipyards and armouries, which operated an incredible production line, way ahead of its time. At its peak the yards were capable of producing a ship a day and in 1574 a complete galley was built during a banquet lunch given for King Henry III of France, which featured extraordinary sculptures made of sugar and had gold dust sprinkled over the food. This sparked a fashion among Venetian nobility for entertaining guests with lavishness bordering on the obscene, and it became the fashion to garnish every dish with gold dust. It was not uncommon to spend 400–500 ducats on such entertainment. (In Elizabethan England, one ducat was equivalent to one crown or 25p, at a time when a servant's salary was no more than £2 per year.)

The biggest party of them all was *carnevale*, a time of masked balls and feasting in the run up to Lent, culminating in martedì grasso (mardi gras or pancake day). Since fatty foods were forbidden for the 40 days of Lent, people would eat as much as they could beforehand! One of the typical treats would have been the irresistible fritelle (doughnuts) filled with zabaione custard. These are still made in the wonderful Rosa Salva patisserie just off St Mark's Square. In the 18th century *carnevale* ran for a full six months from October to April, with only a break for Christmas!

The End of an Era

The glory days of Venice came to an end in 1797 when Napoleon Bonaparte overran Venice and handed it over to Austria under the treaty of Campo Formio. In 1802 the last doge Lodovico Manin died, ending a direct and unbroken succession of 120 doges over a period of 1,100 years, during which Venice had avoided capture or the overthrow of its government. With Austrian rule, *carnevale* dwindled and was ultimately banned under Mussolini in the 1930s. It was only in 1979 that it was revived, and once again the world began to flock to Venice to revel in a fortnight of food and parties.

Bereft of spices and under the influence of Austria, Venetians began to be pleased with simpler foods. By the 19th century, a typical Venetian invitation to dinner would be 'venga a mangiar quattro risi con me', 'come and eat rice with me' (or more literally 'come and eat four grains of rice with me') and so modern day Venetian cooking with its simple fish dishes, *cicchetti* and risotto, is a long way from the rich and sensual dishes of its past.

Venetian Recipes Found...

There is a dichotomy between the simplicity of the modern Venetian kitchen and the exotic, spice-filled cooking of the past, and Giancarlo and I have become fascinated by both. Venice may have lost the splendour and sensuality, even much of the sexiness, of its food after the spices left but the more Giancarlo and I delved, we began to discover a new wave of Venetian chefs equally keen to explore the spices of ancient times alongside contemporary influences from the East. For example, dishes such as clams in ginger broth, and turbot with juniper berries and pepper, hark back to the past, yet have a contemporary simplicity to them.

Then a friend introduced us to restaurateur Sergio Fragiacomo of Bistrot de Venise, in the old part of the city, not far from Piazza San Marco. Sergio, like us, has become fascinated by the historical cooking of Venice. Some of the food he serves is inspired by recipes from *Libro per Cuoco*, a cookbook by an anonymous Venetian chef in the 14th century known as the Anonimo Veneziano. When you taste these dishes the flavours seem utterly new, and it was the discovery of this old cookbook and the Bistrot de Venise that really shaped my ideas for this book. The more I researched and experimented, the more I became obsessed with the idea of discovering the lost food of the decadent past, and bringing it back to the table in the modern kitchen.

The Anonimo Veneziano

The original of the remarkable 14th century work *Libro per Cuoco* (*Book for Cook*), as this Venetian cookbook has become known, is in Rome at the Biblioteca Casanatense, although online versions in the Venetian dialect and English also exist (see Bibliography). Giancarlo and I went to Rome to see the book first-hand. Measuring no more than 12 x 8 cm (5 x 3¼ in) and written by hand in brown ink, it was incredible to touch the pages that were created so many centuries ago. It was clearly a book intended for the cooks to the rich of Venice as the recipes are full of spices, almonds, oranges, parsley, cheese, milk, cream, eggs and agresta, or verjuice as we now know it. The pasta is not as we would recognise it today and there was no potato, chilli or olive oil, and not yet much sugar, so the sweetness was provided by honey. The book describes the way that different groups of spices would be blended to give a sweet or strong flavour:

'Fine spices for all things.' This was a blend of pepper, cinnamon, ginger, cloves and saffron.

'Sweet spices, enough for many good and fine things. The best fine sweet spices that you can make.' A mixture of cloves, ginger, cinnamon and Indian bay leaves that was 'marvellously good' for fish, broths and sauces.

'Black and strong spices for many sauces.' This blend was made from cloves, black pepper, long pepper and nutmeg.

Poring over the English translation of the book, I felt like an alchemist pounding the spices together in my pestle and mortar. Whenever I make them I feel in touch with the past as I concoct potions to soothe and heal my guests. The flavours aren't like anything I know, though they are something akin to a mild curry or tagine – spicy but gentle – and they always seem to delight everyone who tries them. Since there are often no exact measurements, it was exciting, if a little bewildering, to try adding the various concoctions of sweet, strong and spicy to different foods. Luckily for us, Giancarlo was invited to go and work at Bistrot de Venise where he learnt how they had interpreted the recipes, and I have included the best of our subsequent results in this book.

Also fascinating to read are *The Opera of Bartolomeo Scappi*, which was published in 1570 and is a collection of recipes from the personal cook to two popes, and Maestro Martino's *Libro de Arte Coquinaria (The Art of Cooking)*, which was written around 1465 and considered to be a seminal work on Italian gastronomy. It is from Martino, a Renaissance cook from Como, that we get the delicious Garlic Sauce for Meat, found on page 219.

Food, Music and Love

Some Useful Tips

Food found its way into the Venetian theatre with the famous and influential 18th-century playwright Carlo Goldini mentioning recipes, such as Sweet and Sour Sardines (see page 43), in many of his plays. And Venetians loved to sing about food. Just as the gondoliers famously used to sing to amuse themselves and their passengers, often taking it in turns with different verses, so too did the market stallholders, who sang of their wares; and the fishwives, who apparently sang the songs of Tasso the poet out to sea, as they waited for their husbands to return to the coast. When the men were near enough to the coast to hear, they too sang out to reassure the women they were safe and on their way home.

One of the city's most famous – or infamous – sons, of course, is Casanova, who in his memoirs detailed his eating habits, as well as his other more famous talents. He is known to have eaten large amounts of oysters, starting the suggestion that they are an aphrodisiac, and he also liked to eat cheese with his lovers. To give him enough energy for a night on the town, he would have hot chocolate, and a salad of cooked egg whites with a dressing made of Lucca olive oil and Four Thieves Vinegar. He also details his visits to Florian's coffee house to enjoy chocolate, sweet wine and biscuits. In fact, when he was in jail, it was with the help of a plate of macaroni on top of a bible that he was able to smuggle a metal spike to another inmate so that they could make their daring escape.

The restaurants of Venice are inevitably packed, so do your research (we have helped with a list of our favourite restaurants in the back of this book; see pages 264–65) and make reservations in advance, as you can't expect to walk in and find a table in the most popular places.

During the period between Christmas and *carnevale*, Venice is much less crowded, so it is a good time to get around easily. However, quite a few restaurants are closed during this time, so if there is somewhere you really want to visit do check that they will be open.

Though the best restaurants are expensive, save up for these bigger splurges by eating *cicchetti* (Italian tapas) on other evenings.

Local wine from the Veneto is not expensive. Ask for a carafe or a calice of vino locale.

And take comfortable shoes: Venice is for walking and talking, as well as eating! Occasionally in winter the water level in the lagoon rises and floods the lower levels of Venice. It is called *acqua alta*, meaning high water and a few hours before the tide comes in an alarm goes off. It is a scary sound that echoes around the streets, often in the middle of the night. You have to count the alarms after the first whining sounds: each one represents ten centimetres of flood water, so you know if you need waterproof shoes, wellies or full-on waders. In my meeting with pasticceria Rosa Salva we got up from the boardroom table and I discovered we were all wearing smart business attire and green wellies.

bibliotheca SelfCheck System

BALTIMORE COUNTY PUBLIC LIBRARY

Randallstown Branch
410-887-0770
www.bcpl.info

Customer ID: **********7179

Items that you checked out

Title. Cook me* : *please : 30 dishes/3 ways,
90 lip-smacking recipes!
ID: 31183215004687
Due: Wednesday, November 22, 2023

Title: Make it yours with Mimi G : a sewist's
guide to a custom wardrobe
ID. 31183214491729
Due: Wednesday, November 22, 2023

Title: Recipes from Venice
ID: 31183214735083
Due: Wednesday, November 22, 2023

Total items: 3
Account balance: $0.00
Checked out: 3
Messages:
Patron status is ok.
11/1/2023 4:18 PM

Free to Be All In
Late fees no longer assessed for over due
items
Ask for details or visit bcpl.info

Shelf Help 410-494-9063
www.bcpl.info

At the Bar

On a hot sunny day, centuries ago, Venetians would gather beneath the shade of the *campanile* located in St Mark's Square and drink wine together. The wine was served on top of a barrel acting as a portable table which could be moved as the sun moved. Since the glass of wine was always kept out of direct sunlight it became known as an *ombra*, meaning a 'shade' of wine, and this term still exists today. Small bites known as *cicchetti*, were served with the wine, and when the barmen and barrels moved into permanent establishments the bars became known as *bacari*.

Bacari are usually attended for an aperitif before dinner; it is said a Venetian drinks a spritz, between 6 and 8 pm and a tourist at any other time. It marks of the end of the working day.

Antipasti dishes served in restaurants are often wonderful plates of the freshest seafood or crispy, salty *fritto misto*, and are irresistible with a chilled glass of Prosecco.

Cloudy Prosecco

I watched with pleasant surprise as workmen from a nearby building came into a locals' bar in one of the backstreets of Venice and drank a Prosecco at around 11.30 am from a delicate flute held in their scarred and dusty builders' hands. As they get older, I was told, they progress on to a coffee with sambuca to kick-start the day!

Venice is the homeland of Prosecco and it is served as an aperitif, with fish or fried foods when it cuts through the fat beautifully. Typically the Prosecco here is made in the Veneto region; my favourite version is very dry and is bottled 'on the lees' meaning the dead yeast is retained inside the bottle. This can make it cloudy if the sediment is disturbed. It is light at 11% so great for a midday tipple, available by the glass or carafe (calice). Ask for Prosecco col fondo for the cloudy version, or simply 'Prosecco' for the clear, traditional sparkling wine.

Spritz

You won't be able to travel far in Venice without seeing someone enjoying a bright orange cocktail known as a spritz. It is the most typical Venetian aperitif. Born in Venice at the time of Austrian domination, it is a blend of a quarter Aperol or Campari (or occasionally a similar drier drink known as Select) and three quarters Prosecco topped up with a splash of soda water. Serve it over ice and a slice of orange.

Bellini

Although served all over the world this fantastically famous drink was one of Giuseppe Cipriani's, the founder of the iconic Harry's Bar, inventions. According to his son Arrigo, he thought of it in the thirties but didn't name it until 1948 when there was an exhibition of Giovanni Bellini's paintings. Originally it was only made in summer from fresh white peaches and they employed a man just to stone and squeeze the peach flesh by hand. Nowadays they use white peach purée from France, which can easily be bought online.

METHOD

To make a Bellini, chill the white peach purée so that it is very cold. Mix one part purée to three parts Prosecco in a jug with a long spoon and then pour into chilled glasses. At Harry's Bar they use thin straight tumblers that look great with the peachy foam inside. That's it. Serve straight away and enjoy.

Madeira

This toffee-like aromatic sweet wine is no longer common in the bars of Venice but it was a popular and important trading commodity in the past. England bought tons of it from the Venetians, often swapping it for wool. The Venetian merchants had in turn bought it from the island of Madeira. It travelled well and survived long journeys on galley ships. In fact, it was discovered that the wine actually improved after being rocked about for months on a hot ship and thus did its value. Madeira is made from the malvasia grape and at one point any sweet wine was known as malvasia and wine shops were known as malvasie. Apparently the Duke of Clarence died in a barrel of malmsey Madeira after being tried for treason against his brother. We've included it in the book as it was so significant in the past and we feel it deserves further popularity. Drink it on its own, with ice, a slice of orange and some raspberries, or use it to soak prunes or figs in (see page 253).

Cherry Wine

A glass of sweet, spiced wine was thought to encourage an appetite in 15th- and 16th-century Venice and was often served as an aperitif. According to 17th-century writer Giovanni Del Turco, cherry-flavoured wine could be made by soaking cherries with wine for eight days, and in the 14th century cookbook written by the Anonimo Veneziano – the anonymous Venetian – wine was often flavoured with cinnamon, ginger and honey. We have made our version of cherry wine (see page 249) to work in just a day if the cherries are good. You can strain off the wine and drink this as an aperitif as the Venetians did and then eat the heavenly combination of boozy cherries with Almond Ice Cream afterwards (see page 255) or make cherry coulis for the Almond-filled Doughnuts on page 226.

POLPETTINE DI CARNE

Little Meat Patties

SERVES 10–12 (MAKES AROUND 32 PATTIES)

These are classic *cicchetti*; they are sold in most of the *bacari* in Venice and vary from place to place. Our favourites are made by the grandmother at the tiny Osteria alla Scuela restaurant in the Castello district of Venice. She makes them every day and her secret is to include a little cooked potato, which makes them soft and moist to eat rather than dry and hard. In ancient books there are all sorts of recipes for *polpette* (large meatballs) and *polpettine* (little meatballs) *di carne*, which have been made for centuries with flavourings such as candied fruits, rum, rosewater and spices. Serve them as they are or toss them together with homemade tomato sauce and spaghetti.

METHOD

Boil the potatoes in their skins and when tender drain. Spear them with a fork and peel off the skin with a knife. Now mash them in a large bowl. Add the rest of the *polpette* ingredients and use your hands to mix everything together until well blended. Take a piece of the mixture and roll it into a walnut-size ball, then flatten it into a patty shape, and then fry this in a little oil until cooked. Taste and adjust the seasoning as necessary; this way you won't make and fry all your *polpette* and then realise you haven't added enough salt! When you are happy with the flavour, make up the rest of the patties. Each one should weigh around 30 g (1 oz).

Heat the oil in a deep-fat fryer or a high-sided frying pan until it is around 175°C (345°F) or hot enough to make a small piece of bread sizzle as soon as it enters the fat. Prepare the flour, egg and breadcrumbs in three separate bowls. Dip each patty first into the flour and tap off the excess, then into the egg and finally the breadcrumbs, gently pressing them in. If you run out of egg, add a dash of milk to the bowl. Gently put the patties into the hot oil in batches so the fryer isn't overcrowded and fry for around 5 minutes until dark golden brown and cooked through. Drain on paper towels and cut one open to check it is cooked through to the middle. Eat as soon as they are cool enough to touch.

The patties can be reheated in a warm oven if you want to make them in advance. They also freeze well.

FOR THE *POLPETTINE*

300 g (10½ oz) potatoes

500 g (1 lb 2 oz/2 cups) lean minced (ground) beef

50 g (1¾ oz) onions, very finely chopped

½ tsp finely grated nutmeg

½ tsp ground cinnamon (optional)

Salt and freshly ground black pepper

2 tbsp parsley, finely chopped

1 small garlic clove, finely chopped

50 g (1¾ oz) Parmesan, finely grated

Finely grated zest of ½ lemon

TO COAT THE *POLPETTE*

4 tbsp '00' or plain (all-purpose) flour

1 large egg, beaten

60 g (2 oz/⅔ cup) dry breadcrumbs

Sunflower oil for deep-frying

POLPETTE DI MELANZANE

Aubergine Balls

SERVES 6–8 (MAKES 24 BALLS)

At Al Mercà, a popular tiny *bacaro* near the Rialto, you can see pyramids of breadcrumbed patties made from beef, aubergine (eggplant) or tuna; one for every taste and usually taken with a Spritz. These are great on their own as *cicchetti* or with tomato sauce for a more substantial meal and as an alternative to meatballs. Not so Venetian, but if you want to serve them with a dip, Greek yoghurt mixed with chopped cucumber would be ideal.

METHOD

Preheat the oven to 200°C (400°F/Gas 6). Put the aubergine slices on an oven rack over a baking tray. Brush the slices lightly with 2 tablespoons of the olive oil and bake for 20–25 minutes or until they look dry and slightly browned. Set aside to cool. Blend the aubergine with the potato and mint in a food processor to a coarse paste or chop finely together by hand, then transfer to a large bowl. Heat the remaining olive oil in a frying pan over a medium heat and cook the onion for 5–7 minutes or until soft and translucent. Add the garlic and chilli (according to taste) for the last couple of minutes. Remove from the heat and allow to cool. Stir in the cheese.

Meanwhile, prepare the polpette coating following the same instructions to coat the *Polpettine di Carne* opposite. Heat the oil in a deep-fat fryer or a high-sided frying pan until it is around 175°C (345°F) or hot enough to make a piece of bread sizzle as soon as it enters the fat.

Combine the cooled onion and cheese mixture with the aubergine mixture and season to taste. Make one ball to test the flavour. Take a piece of the mixture and roll it into a walnut-size ball; this is easier if you wet your fingers with cold water first. To coat it follow the instructions for coating the *Polpettine di Carne* opposite. Gently put the ball into the hot oil, and fry for 4–5 minutes until golden brown and cooked through. Drain on paper towels, cut open to check it is cooked to the middle and eat as soon as it is cool enough to touch. If necessary, adjust the seasoning and mint in the aubergine mixture and cook another test ball until you are happy with the flavour, then make and fry the rest of the balls.

FOR THE *POLPETTE*

2 aubergines (eggplants), cut into 1 cm (½ in) thick round slices

4 tbsp extra virgin olive oil

150 g (5½ oz) potatoes, cooked and peeled as in Little Meat Patties (opposite)

3 tbsp mint leaves, finely chopped

1 medium onion, finely chopped

1 garlic clove, finely chopped

½ red chilli, finely chopped

30 g (1 oz) Parmesan or grana padano, finely grated

Salt and freshly ground black pepper

TO COAT THE *POLPETTE*

4 tbsp '00' or plain (all-purpose) flour

1 large egg, beaten

60 g (2 oz/⅔ cup) dry breadcrumbs

Sunflower oil for deep-frying

POLPETTINE DI TONNO

Tuna Patties

SERVES 6

If you struggle to find sustainable tuna, you can also make these patties with sardines, mackerel or pilchards. Living far from the sea I use tinned fish either in oil or brine, which I find works really well. You can flavour the patties with either curry powder or lemon zest, but don't use both together. For a quick dip, you can mix a little curry powder in with the mayonnaise.

METHOD

Mix together in a large bowl the fish, potatoes, parsley, lemon zest or curry powder, and seasoning. Fry the onion in the oil over a medium heat for 5–7 minutes until soft. Add the potato and fish mixture to the pan and stir through until well combined, then leave to cool.

To make and fry the patties, follow the same instructions in the Little Meat Patties method (see page 22).

Serve on their own, with a squeeze of lemon or with some mayonnaise mixed with a little curry powder to taste, if using.

A NOTE ABOUT BREADCRUMBS

Breadcrumbs are made (by blitzing in a food processor) either soft from a fresh loaf or dry from one that has become stale.

If you have only fresh soft bread and you want dry breadcrumbs, break up the loaf into egg-sized chunks and put them into an oven preheated to 180°C (350°F/Gas 4) for around 15 minutes to crisp up. Next pulse the chunks in a food processor to the desired texture (for very fine dust, remove the breadcrumbs from the processor and rub them through a sieve). Alternatively, I like to use Japanese panko breadcrumbs, as they are crisp and don't seem to absorb too much oil, and can be bought ready-made from most supermarkets.

However, if you want wet, soft breadcrumbs and all your bread is hard, soak stale bread in milk and when it is soft squeeze out the excess milk before transferring to the food processor.

Breadcrumbs can be frozen; I find keeping little bags of them in my freezer very useful.

Giancarlo likes to blitz herbs and garlic into his breadcrumbs so that they turn green and are well flavoured before use.

FOR THE *POLPETTINE*

225 g (8 oz) tinned tuna (net weight, drained of oil or water)

300 g (10½ oz/1⅓ cups) potatoes, cooked and mashed as in Little Meat Patties (see page 22)

4 tbsp parsley, finely chopped

Finely grated zest of ½–1 lemon or 2 tsp curry powder

Salt and freshly ground black pepper

1 medium onion, finely chopped

3 tbsp extra virgin olive oil

TO COAT THE *POLPETTE*

4 tbsp '00' or plain (all-purpose) flour

1 large egg, beaten

60 g (2 oz/⅔ cup) dry breadcrumbs

Sunflower oil for deep-frying

Juice of 1 lemon, to serve (optional)

Mayonnaise, to serve (optional)

Curry powder, to taste (optional)

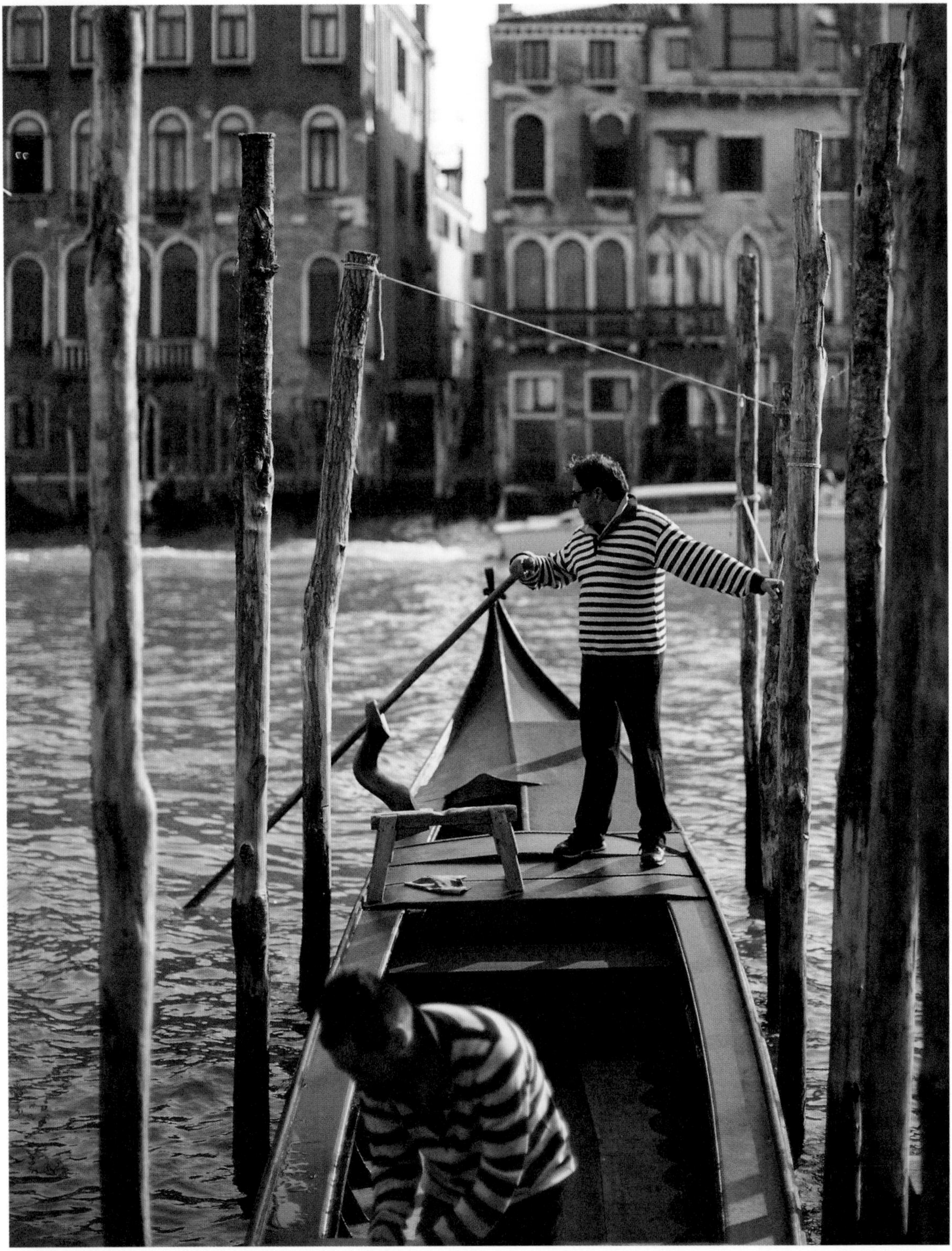

TRAMEZZINI

Sandwiches

The first time I visited Venice in my twenties I was really there to see the art. I should have known then my heart and interests really lay with Venice's food rather than her paintings. I can't remember a single painting or sculpture but I can remember the *bacari* where they served overstuffed sandwiches called *tramezzini*. On a student budget it meant I could fill my ever-hungry stomach with these filling little morsels. Each one appeared to be made with love and care as they still do today in the less touristy spots. Interesting fillings include artichokes that ooze their marinating oil as you bite into them, bitter leaves of radicchio with sweet crab meat or flakes of tuna with boiled egg and mayonnaise.

At the patisserie Rosa Salva they are made with a buttery béchamel instead of the mayonnaise.

TO MAKE TRAMEZZINI

Choose white bread that is firm in texture, a best quality medium-sliced loaf should do it. Don't use any butter, just spread each slice generously with mayonnaise. Lay on the fillings, going overboard in the centre so the whole thing will be ridiculously overstuffed. Season well with salt and pepper and close up the sandwiches, pressing down around the crusts. Slice off all the crusts and cut into two triangles. If you are not eating them straight away, store under a slightly damp tea towel in the refrigerator or cover with cling film (plastic wrap).

OUR FAVOURITE FILLINGS ARE:

Artichoke, thinly sliced ham and mayonnaise

White crab meat and radicchio or bitter lettuce

Asparagus and sliced boiled egg

Porchetta (a salty, herby roast pork) and grilled sliced aubergine (eggplant)

Smoked salmon and hard-boiled egg

Spinach, finely chopped and mixed with mayonnaise, and thinly sliced smoked ham

Cooked tuna fillets under oil, hard-boiled egg and capers

Smoked ham and chopped gherkin

PARMESAN AND
RICOTTA PESTO
WITH ASPARAGUS
AND ALMOND
FLAKES

POMEGRANATE
AND GINGER
SAUCE WITH BRIE

RICOTTA
AND WALNUT
CROSTINI

PARMESAN AND
RICOTTA PESTO
WITH BROAD
BEANS

SWEET CRAB
MEAT AND
RADICCHIO

CROSTINI E PANINI

Toasted Bread and Little Filled Rolls

Little rounds of toasted bread and miniature bread rolls are topped and filled with imaginative ingredients and sold in the *bacari* all over Venice. Made with love and care, recipes vary hugely and reflect the personality of the *bacaro*. We have seen sea urchin on shredded lettuce, eggs with truffled cream and pink peppercorns, inventive ideas with nuts and seeds, as well as the clever use of local seafood. If you don't eat bread, sliced, toasted polenta, is ideal for a base, or thinly sliced, grilled courgettes (zucchini) and aubergines (eggplants) can be rolled around the fillings.

CROSTINI DI RICOTTA E NOCI

Ricotta and Walnut Crostini

SERVES 6

At the famous *bacaro* Cantinone già Schiavi, the *cicchetti* are so popular that Alessandra de Respinis, the owner, has written a little book of her favourite combinations entitled *Cicchettario*. Our favourite fillings here were creamy tuna mayonnaise made with brandy and topped with strips of leeks; grilled aubergine (eggplant) with stracchino cheese; walnut and Parmesan pesto on ricotta with redcurrants; and chestnut pesto, robiola cheese and courgette (zucchini). She also uses hard-boiled eggs as vessels for her delicious concoctions.

TO MAKE CROSTINI

Choose a small sourdough loaf or a French baguette and cut into slices around 2 cm (¾ in) thick. Bake at 200°C (400°F/Gas 6) on a rack in an oven for a few minutes until just golden. Remove from the oven and allow to cool on the rack. Then spread with your favourite topping and serve. Don't make them too far in advance or they will become soggy. Alternatively, use cooled, firm polenta and toast or fry squares of it (see page 111) before adding your topping. These polenta squares are frequently topped with Baccalà Mantecato, a creamy mousse made from salted dried cod (see pages 180–81).

TO MAKE THE PESTO

Blend together in a food processor the walnuts, Parmesan, garlic and enough oil to make the mixture runny; do not over-blend as it should still have a slightly rough texture. Season to taste. Spread a generous tablespoon of ricotta over each crostini and drizzle over the pesto. Top with redcurrants.

6 crostini

6 generous tbsp ricotta

Handful of redcurrants

FOR THE PESTO

30 g (1 oz/¼ cup) walnuts

30 g (1 oz/¼ cup) Parmesan, finely grated

¼ garlic clove

Extra virgin olive oil

Salt and freshly ground black pepper

CREMA DI PARMIGIANO E RICOTTA

Parmesan and Ricotta Pesto for Crostini

MAKES 300 G (10½ OZ), ENOUGH FOR 15–20 SLICES OF TOASTED BAGUETTE

This brilliantly useful pesto couldn't be easier to make and can be spread over hot toast, cooled crostini or stirred into pasta or risotto. We use it to top crostini and then put whatever vegetables we have over the top for canapés or a quick lunch.

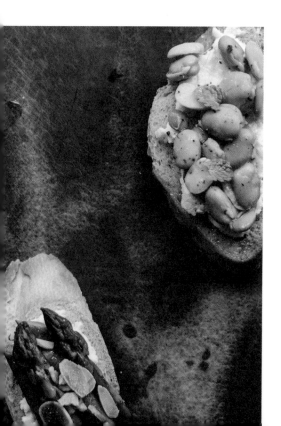

METHOD

Mix the cheeses together with the oil and season to taste. Use straight away or you can store the pesto in the refrigerator for up to a week. Spread onto hot toast or cooled crostini (see opposite) and top with vegetables cut to fit on the toasts. Steamed asparagus is lovely with toasted almonds on top or try cooked shelled broad (fava) beans.

50 g (1¾ oz) Parmesan, finely grated

150 g (5½ oz/ ⅔ cup) mascarpone

100 g (3½ oz/ generous ⅓ cup) ricotta

2 tsp extra virgin olive oil

Fine salt and freshly ground black pepper

QUADRATI DI POLENTA A SCACCHI

Black and White Polenta Squares

Set polenta cut into shapes makes an easy alternative to bread for *cicchetti* and canapés. The polenta can be white, yellow, flavoured with rosemary (see page 111) or coloured with cuttlefish ink. Black polenta is made by adding cuttlefish ink to the polenta as it is being cooked; add spoonfuls of ink until you have the right density of colour. The better quality of ink you buy (either online or from an Italian deli), the less ink you will need. It is available in jars or sachets. Cut the black set polenta into squares and lay on the plate with squares of white polenta for a dramatic chequerboard effect.

Excellent combinations to eat with black polenta are spoonfuls of Creamy Salt Cod (see pages 180–81) or make a cream from Horseradish Sauce (see page 169) mixed with ricotta and top it with flakes of golden smoked fish and black pepper.

Serve your polenta *cicchetti* at room temperature with chilled glasses of Prosecco.

CARNE SALATA

Salted Beef

MAKES AROUND 800 G (1 LB 12 OZ) CURED BEEF

This is a typical recipe from Trentino Alto Adige, the mountainous region north-west of Venice, but it is easy to make at home. Traditionally made from a *fesa* – the topside – of beef; it is cured with salt and herbs for ten days and served thinly sliced. The topside should be trimmed of any fat and sinew and be very lean. Francesco Zorzetto, owner of the *barco* La Cantina, makes a wonderful version that his customers visit him for. He serves it on crostini (see page 32) with a julienne of horseradish and some crumbled goat's cheese. I think the spicier flavour and firm texture is more interesting than the normal Raw Beef Salad (see page 54), but like carpaccio this beef is also perfect topped with Parmesan shavings, rocket (arugula) and a lemon and olive oil dressing.

METHOD

Put the bay leaves, garlic, juniper berries, peppercorns and rosemary into a pestle and mortar and bash together to form a rough paste, then add the salt and stir through. Coat the meat all over with the flavoured salt and place it into a container just bigger than the piece of beef. Weigh the meat down by placing a heavy UHT juice box or small clean brick well covered in cling film (plastic wrap) on top of it. Cover and leave in the refrigerator for 10 days until it is firm to the touch. Every day, turn the meat and pour away any liquid from the container.

Wash the meat briefly to get rid of any remaining salty brine and pat dry. Don't worry if a few spices remain as it gives texture and looks attractive. The outside will be saltier than the inside, so don't panic on the first tasting. Slice thinly and serve with rocket, Parmesan shavings, a squeeze of lemon and a drizzle of olive oil. The beef can also be cut into 5 mm (¼ in) slices and cooked briefly in a frying pan and served hot. The rest can be tightly covered in cling film (plastic wrap) and stored in the refrigerator for up to 2 weeks.

6 bay leaves, roughly chopped

5 garlic cloves, peeled

15 juniper berries

15 black peppercorns

3 sprigs of rosemary

75 g (2½ oz/¼ cup) coarse sea salt

1 × 1 kg (2 lb 4 oz) fesa or sirloin, trimmed of any fat and skin

POMODORI SECCHI CON MOZZARELLA E BASILICO

Sun-dried Tomato with Mozzarella and Basil

William Sfrizzo, a seller of sun-dried (bell) peppers and tomatoes in the Rialto market was so proud of his product that he showed us his iPad footage taken in Sicily where you can see literally acres of tomatoes lying open on racks in the sun. It takes just three days to dry them after they are washed in salt. The scale and yet the low-tech approach that has worked for probably centuries was incredible to see. The flavour was even better, sweet and savoury with the moreish hit of umami to boot.

William told us that you could use them for antipasti dressed with oil and vinegar, and stacked on small chunks of mozzarella and basil leaves – or whizz them up into a sauce and pour over sliced mozzarella or cooked fish. Stock up on bags of them when you are abroad and keep them in the cupboard until you need them. They are miles better than anything in oil from a jar.

METHOD

To bring the dried tomatoes back to life, put 100 g (3½ oz) into 2 litres (68 fl oz/8½ cups) boiling water with 3 tablespoons of white wine vinegar. Cook them for 6–10 minutes or until the salty taste has gone. Stir occasionally but don't let them break up. Drain them, rinse and drain again. Squeeze them gently between two sheets of paper towels, pressing down on the top for a couple of minutes. Put them in extra virgin olive oil with a splash of white or red wine vinegar and a crushed garlic clove. Make sure they are always submerged in the oil. I keep mine in a jar or plastic container with a lid. They are ready to eat after a day but will keep in the refrigerator for up to 10 days.

For dried peppers, do the same as above but boil for just 1½–2 minutes and store as above.

Saor

Saor is Venetian dialect from *sapore* meaning 'flavour', in this sense a sweet and sour flavour. This is one of the oldest cooking techniques, dating back at least to the 1300s if not before, and is still popular in Venice today. Since the dish contains a fair amount of vinegar, it was originally used as a method of preserving fish to take on sea voyages. A base of slow-cooked onions (usually double the quantity of onions to fish) and vinegar is used, and various ingredients can be added to this such as sardines, aubergines (eggplants), pumpkin and beans such as borlotti (cranberry) or cannellini. During the Renaissance, a winter version was developed with the addition of sultanas and pine nuts to add sweetness.

CIPOLLE IN SAOR

Sweet and Sour Onions

MAKES 1 KG (2 LB 4 OZ)

Venetians love the sweet and sour flavour of these onions and add them to all sorts of foods. Once you have made them you can enjoy them with grilled meats and cheeses, or see the recipes for Pumpkin in Saor (see page 177).

METHOD

In a large saucepan, cook the onions with the oil, salt and bay leaves for 35–40 minutes over a very low heat. Add the vinegar and sugar and continue to cook for 5 minutes. Remove from the heat and cool to room temperature.

Store any leftover onions in a sealed contained in the refrigerator for up to 7 days.

1 kg (2 lb 4 oz) white onions, sliced into half moons (see page 46)

120 ml (4 fl oz/ ½ cup) olive oil

2 tsp salt, to taste

2 bay leaves

4 tbsp white wine vinegar

1 tsp caster (superfine) sugar

Sweet and Sour Sardines with Onions, Pine Nuts and Raisins

SERVES 8–10

Sarde in Saor was mentioned in a few of Carlo Goldoni's plays, which helped spread its popularity, and is traditionally eaten during the Redentore celebration on the third Saturday of July. Almost every *bacaro* and restaurant serves its own version of the dish, either on polenta or crostini. This is Sabrina Busato's recipe, a young Venetian girl who learnt it from her grandmother.

METHOD

If the sardines have scales, scrape them off using a dinner knife under running water. With a sharp knife, remove the heads, from just behind the gills, and tails of the sardines. Using scissors, cut down the belly of each fish, open out and remove the guts. Use your fingers and thumbs to push away the spines and discard. Pull out the dorsal fin – this will remove the remnants of the backbone too. Wash the sardines and dry on paper towels.

Heat the oil in a large frying pan and, when the oil is hot, fry the sardines, in batches if necessary, for about 2–5 minutes on each side, depending on thickness, until just firm to the touch. They should be slightly underdone rather than overcooked. Carefully lift the sardines from the pan, keeping them whole, and lay in a dish. Leave the remaining oil in the pan. Taste a little piece of one of the sardines and add salt if necessary. If the fish are really fresh, they are full of salty seawater so you won't need to.

In the same pan, cook the onion and bay leaf over a gentle heat for around 10 minutes so that the onion softens but does not take on any colour. Pour in the vinegar and continue to cook for 5 minutes. Add the wine and cook for 5 more minutes. Remove the onion from the pan with a pair of tongs and lay on top of the sardines. (If your dish is small or you are doing double this quantity, you can layer up the sardines and onions.) Discard the pan juices. Scatter the sultanas and pine nuts over the onions. Cover the dish with cling film (plastic wrap) and leave in the refrigerator for at least 2 days (Sabrina suggests 5 days). The sardines will keep for up to 10 days and are usually served on or with Black and White Polenta Squares (see page 34). Don't worry about keeping the fish whole; they will break up as you take a serving.

1 kg (2 lb 4 oz) sardines

120 ml (4 fl oz/ ½ cup) sunflower oil

Salt, to taste

1 large white onion (approximately 300 g (10½ oz) sliced into half moons (see page 46)

1 bay leaf (optional)

100 ml (3½ fl oz/ ½ cup) white wine vinegar

100 ml (3½ fl oz/ ½ cup) white wine

30 g (1 oz) sultanas (golden raisins)

30 g (1 oz/¼ cup) pine nuts

CISAME DE PESSE

Sole and Prawns in Saor

SERVES 12–14

This recipe follows in the tradition of the Sweet and Sour Sardines (see page 44) and is vivid yellow in colour from the use of saffron. The original recipe, 'A sweet and sour dish of whichever fish you want', comes from *Libro per Cuoco* by the Anonimo Veneziano: 'Take the fish and fry it. Take onions, which have been boiled a little and chopped finely, and fry them well. Then take vinegar and water and whole peeled almonds, currants, strong spices and a little honey and put everything to boil together (with the onions) and put it above the (fried) fish.'

The clever crew at restaurant Bistrot de Venise have taken that brief description and worked it up into a really splendid first course where piles of soft, saffron-yellow onions sit atop delicate sole and fat pink prawns.

2 kg (4 lb 8 oz) white onions

150 ml (5 fl oz/ ⅔ cup) extra virgin olive oil

50 g (1¾ oz) fresh ginger, peeled and roughly sliced

500 ml (17 fl oz/ generous 2 cups) white wine vinegar

300 ml (10 fl oz/ 1¼ cups) white wine

½ tsp saffron strands

2 tsp ground turmeric

2 tsp fine salt, plus extra for seasoning

2 tbsp caster (superfine) sugar

50 g (1¾ oz/ ½ cup) flaked (slivered) almonds

100 g (3½ oz/scant 1 cup) pine nuts

200 g (7 oz/ 1⅔ cups) sultanas (golden raisins)

Sunflower oil for deep-frying

500 g (1 lb 2 oz) lemon sole, skinned, boned and each fillet cut into thirds

500 g (1 lb 2 oz) raw medium prawns (shrimp), peeled and deveined

'00' or plain (all-purpose) flour for dusting

METHOD

Peel the onions and cut them in half from root to tip. Place one half of the onion flat side down, cut off the root, trim the tip and slice again from root to tip to form 3 mm (⅛ in) thick half-moon slices. Repeat with the other half and then do this for all the onions. Heat the olive oil in a large frying pan and fry the onions for around 30 minutes over a very low heat so that they cook gently and do not take on any colour. Meanwhile, put the ginger, vinegar and white wine together in a saucepan and bring to the boil. Simmer for 5 minutes and then whisk in the saffron, turmeric, salt and sugar. Remove from the heat and set aside to infuse. After 30 minutes, discard the ginger and pour the vinegar mixture into the onions along with the almonds, pine nuts and sultanas. Continue to cook for another 10 minutes or until the onions are really soft.

Add enough sunflower oil to a large high-sided frying pan or a deep-fat fryer to deep-fry the seafood. Heat the oil to around 175°C (345°F) or when hot enough to make a small piece of bread sizzle when it hits the fat. Season the fish and prawns lightly and dust with flour. Tap off the excess. Fry in batches for around 1–2 minutes until just firm and just cooked through. Remove the seafood from the oil and drain on paper towels. Arrange in layers in a large lasagne dish with the onions in between. Leave to cool to room temperature. Cover with cling film (plastic wrap) or a lid and chill in the refrigerator for at least 48 hours. They are ready to eat after that time but will last for another 7 days in the refrigerator. Serve at room temperature.

Fritto Misto and the Art of Deep-frying

Crisp just-fried fish or chicken, vegetables or a mixture of the two make up *Fritto Misto*. They are served all over the coastline of Italy throughout the year, depending on the local catch and fresh produce. As well as the typical calamari, a *misto* might include prawns (shrimp), tiny brown shrimps, soft white fish, chicken, artichokes, batons of red (bell) pepper, carrot, courgette (zucchini), aubergine (eggplant) and cauliflower to name but a few. In early summer, courgette flowers are popular and twice a year Venetians go mad for deep-fried soft shell crabs called moeche. They are farmed in the lagoons of Venice and harvested into buckets when they are about to shed their shells and grow the next one. Here they have a blissful end feeding on egg and milk (and I have heard some add Parmesan) before being deep-fried so that they come ready stuffed with a tasty layer of frittata. They are not easy to get abroad, so I leave that particular delicacy to my visits to Venice.

Cesare Benelli at the restaurant Al Covo in Venice explained to me the various types of frying. Sardines, for example, can be *sarde impanate*, which means they are coated in flour, egg and fine breadcrumbs, then fried, or *indorate* meaning 'golden' as they are dipped in flour and/or egg only before being fried. Cesare keeps the fresh fish and seafood in very cold seawater, before coating them in flour and frying them briefly. He thinks the secret is to keep the fish very cold until the moment before they are fried. If he uses a batter for frying, sometimes for vegetables, he uses sparkling water for lightness.

Deep-fried Fish and Vegetables

SERVES 6–8

Marco is the chef in charge of frying at Da Romano, an old traditional restaurant on the pretty island of Burano. He uses '00' flour to coat the fish and vegetables alike, and tosses the *fritto misto* onto absorbent yellow food paper just before they are served on huge oval plates carried by smart waiters in white jackets and bow ties. For a classic batter perfect for frying just fish, see page 53.

Seed oil for deep-frying

500 g (1 lb 2 oz/ 4 cups) '00' flour

400 ml (14 fl oz/ generous 1½ cups) milk or water

500 g (1 lb 2 oz) vegetables (see selection opposite), cut into bite-size batons

500 g (1 lb 2 oz) mixed seafood, cleaned and cut into bite-size pieces

Fine salt, to serve

Lemons, halved, to serve

METHOD

Heat the oil in a large high-sided frying pan or deep-fat fryer to around 175°C (345°F) or hot enough to make a small piece of bread sizzle when it hits the fat. Sift the flour into a large bowl and line another large dish with paper towels. Pour the milk into a third bowl and put the vegetables and seafood, a few at a time, into the milk to soak for 1–2 minutes.

Lift them out with a slotted spoon, giving it a couple of taps to drain most of the liquid. Put them into the flour and toss them with your hands. Gently place them into the hot oil and cook for around 2 minutes or until golden brown. Drain in the bowl lined with paper towels. Scatter with fine salt and serve with some halved lemons.

SARDE INDORATE

Golden Fried Sardines

A plate of just-fried, crisply coated fish so fresh you can still taste the seawater in them, a glass of chilled cloudy Prosecco and a view of the Grand Canal – dining doesn't get much better. Actually my view is currently a postcard of the Grand Canal opposite my desk but the dish is the same. Anchovies, little sardines or sprats are perfect for this, but they must be fresh. In fact, so fresh that they should be straight from the boat or market stall and preferably still in rigor. This dish was cooked for me by our friend and cook Arianna Patron and she called it *scotto ditto*, meaning 'hot fingers', as the fish smells so good you can't wait to eat them and so burn your fingers! Arianna used only flour and told me not to use lemon on the fishes as they just don't need it; she was right.

Any amount of fresh sardines or other fresh small, oily fish

Seed oil for deep-frying

Plate of enough '00' flour to coat the fish

Fine sea salt, to serve

METHOD

Keep the fish ice cold (but not to the point where they freeze) for as long as possible before frying. Remove the heads and spines from the fish but leave the tails intact and wash gently. Drain on paper towels. Heat the oil in a large high-sided frying pan or deep-fat fryer to around 175°C (345°F) or hot enough to make a small piece of bread sizzle when it hits the fat. Dip the fish in the flour and gently tap off the excess. Fry in the hot oil for just 1–2 minutes until cooked through. Drain on paper towels and dust with the salt. Pour a glass of Prosecco and eat the fish while hot.

SARDE IMPANATE

Breadcrumbed Sardines

METHOD

Prepare the sardines as in the Golden Fried Sardines above. Next, dip them into flour, egg and breadcrumbs as in the Little Meat Patties on page 22. Fry as above.

POLLO FRITTO AI SEMI DI FINOCCHIO

Spicy Fennel Seed Chicken

SERVES 2 HUNGRY CHILDREN

While perusing the English translation of the 14th century cookbook *Libro per Cuoco* by the Anonimo Veneziano, I was inspired to use fennel seeds to flavour the chicken I was frying for our children. They loved it and named it 'popcorn chicken', just because it smells like popcorn cooking and comes in bite-size morsels. Not very 14th century or modern Venetian but too good to miss out, the chicken pieces make the perfect *cicchetti* just as they are or slap a few into a bread roll with a good dollop of mayonnaise.

METHOD

Heat the oil in a large high-sided frying pan or deep-fat fryer to around 175°C (345°F) or hot enough to make a small piece of bread sizzle when it enters the fat. Grind the fennel seeds to a fine powder in a pestle and mortar or spice grinder. Mix this into the flour with the salt. Cut the chicken into bite-size nuggets and coat each piece in the flour mixture. Tap off the excess and fry, in batches if necessary, for around 8 minutes until golden. (If you prefer to shallow fry the chicken, beat it flat before cutting and cook for 4 minutes, turning once.) Cut a nugget open to make sure they are cooked through but don't over-fry or they will become dry. Drain on paper towels and serve straight away.

Seed oil for deep-frying

4 tsp fennel seeds

1 heaped tbsp '00' or plain (all-purpose) flour

½ tsp fine salt

2 skinless chicken breasts

PASTELLA PER PESCE FRITTO

Batter for Frying Fish

SERVES 4–6

This batter is ideal for prawns (shrimp) and delicate white fishes that are likely to break up. Like British fish and chips, the point of the batter is to seal the fish so that it steams the fish inside, keeping its moisture and flavour. To achieve the lightest batter, use very cold carbonated water and flour, or as Venetian chef Ada Catto suggests use a level teaspoon of bicarbonate of soda (baking soda) in 1 litre (34 fl oz/4¼ cups) of still water to create the same effect. Ideally, the batter should be left to rest before use. Prawns are amazing cooked this way.

METHOD

Prepare the batter by adding the water to the flour and salt in a large mixing bowl all in one go. Whisk hard to beat out any lumps. The batter should be the consistency of thick soup; adjust with a little more flour or water as necessary. Cover the bowl with cling film (plastic wrap) and chill in the refrigerator for up to 2 hours.

Heat the oil in a large high-sided frying pan or deep-fat fryer to around 175°C (345°F) or hot enough to make a small piece of bread sizzle when it hits the fat. Prepare the fish by cutting it into bite-size pieces, making sure they are no bones left. Peel and devein the prawns, if using, leaving the tails on if you wish. Remove the batter from the refrigerator and dip the fish or prawns into it, letting the excess drip off. Fry the fish in the hot oil and cook for 4–5 minutes until golden brown. Remove a piece and cut it open to check it is cooked through and then remove the fish and drain on paper towels. Season with salt and serve straight away, on their own or with lemon halves.

FOR THE BATTER

250 ml (8½ fl oz/1 cup) sparkling mineral water or cold tap water with 1 tsp bicarbonate of soda (baking soda) added

150 g (5½ oz/1¼ cups) '00' flour

1 tsp fine salt, plus extra to serve

Sunflower oil for frying

500 g (1 lb 2 oz) white fish, skinned and boned, or raw king prawns (jumbo shrimp)

Lemons, halved, to serve (optional)

CARPACCIO DI MANZO

Raw Beef Salad

This internationally famous dish was invented by Giuseppe Cipriani, founder of Harry's Bar, in 1950, which was the year of the great Carpaccio exhibition held in Venice. Giuseppe's son Arrigo told us that the Contessa Amalia Nani Mocenigo, who was a regular at Harry's Bar, had been told by her doctor not to have any cooked meat. Giuseppe, ever the enterprising young man, said he would cut her a plate of thinly sliced raw lean beef. To make it more appetising, he made a sauce from ingredients in his kitchen – mayonnaise, English mustard and Worcestershire sauce. Nowadays the culinary term for anything sliced thinly is carpaccio.

At Harry's Bar they use shell of beef, a tender cut that is full of flavour. Fillet steak is easier to cut but it doesn't match the flavour. Trim a 350 g (12 oz) piece of beef fillet of any visible fat and sinew. Chill in the freezer for 1 hour. Use a razor-sharp knife to slice it as thinly as possible. Lay the slices onto a plate and dress with the sauce alla Giuseppe or top it with rocket (arugula), Parmesan shavings, salt and pepper, and a very good olive oil. Some people add lemon juice but the more flavourings you add, the less you taste the beef.

METHOD

Whisk together the mayonnaise, mustard, Worcestershire sauce and lemon juice. Add 2 tablespoons of milk to thin the sauce and whisk again. It should just coat the back of a spoon; add the remaining milk if necessary. Season to taste and add more Worcestershire sauce as needed. Arrange the sliced beef onto a large plate and pour the sauce over the top in a crosshatch pattern.

FOR THE SAUCE

185 ml (6½ fl oz/ generous ¾ cup) mayonnaise, either homemade or buy the best quality you can

1 tsp English Mustard

1–2 tsp Worcestershire sauce, to taste

1 tsp fresh lemon juice

2–3 tbsp milk

Salt and freshly ground white pepper, to taste

PESCE CRUDO ALLA SALSA DI AGRUMI

Raw Fish Salad with a Citrus Dressing

SERVES 6 AS A STARTER

Raw fish has been eaten in Venice long before any sushi restaurants opened there. Our friend Arianna made me fresh sardines in the simplest way; cleaned and filleted and soaked in a little lemon juice, olive oil and salt. She left them for just five minutes and we ate them with our fingers. Simple and wonderful.

A raw fish platter is served at most restaurants in Venice, as fresh fish is always available. Dressings are pretty simple, ranging from just oil and salt to citrus fruits or tiny piles of wasabi. Plates are decorated with pomegranate seeds, slices of orange and lemon, and nearly always chopped parsley and cracked pepper. At the Carampane restaurant we had swordfish, juicy red prawns (shrimp) that melted on the tongue and a strange looking local shellfish called *canocchie*, the mantis shrimp. In our restaurants, we sell the freshest and most local fish we can find, usually Scottish salmon, fresh mackerel in season or smoked fish such as haddock. At home only serve raw fish if you know it is very fresh indeed.

This is Giancarlo's dressing made from reduced citrus juice and a light olive oil, a Ligurian one is good as it won't detract from the taste of the fish. Before serving, you can also scatter the fish with a handful of parsley, thyme and chervil, finely chopped, if you like. This recipe makes quite a bit of sauce, more than you need for the *Pesce Crudo*, but it is lovely on green salad and keeps well in the refrigerator.

METHOD

Boil the juices in a saucepan and reduce by a third. Remove from the heat and leave to cool down. Add the olive oil, crushed pink peppercorns and sugar to the reduced juice and stir through. Season to taste. Slice the fish as thinly as possible (it helps to chill it briefly in the freezer before you slice it, but don't let it become frozen). Lay the pieces of fish over a plate in a single layer. Stir the dressing and pour over the fish. Scatter over some pink peppercorns to garnish and the rocket leaves. Serve straight away with crusty bread.

Juice of 2 oranges

Juice of 2 lemons

150 ml (5 fl oz/ ⅔ cup) light extra virgin olive oil

1 tsp pink peppercorns, crushed, plus extra to decorate

1 tsp caster (superfine) sugar

Salt and freshly ground black, long or Sichuan peppercorns

500 g (1 lb 2 oz) fresh salmon fillets

A few rocket (arugula) leaves

At the Bakery

Until the last century, bakeries were often the only source of cooking available to Venetians. Only the very wealthy had domestic ovens, the rest would prepare food at home and then take it to the local baker. This was the case not only for bread but also for pies, which might not be the kind of food that immediately springs to mind when you think of Venice. However, there is a long history of pies in Venice, which were often sold as street food: either small, individual ones, or big, impressive ones for portioning up, often coloured with saffron or edible gold dust, to make an impact.

Bread, of course, has always been an integral part of the Italian diet. It is unthinkable to have a meal without bread, and it is always on hand to mop up any delicious juices. Bread rolls and toasted bread are also an important element of *cicchetti*, the Venetian version of tapas (see page 17).

FOCACCINE

Little Salted Bread Rolls

MAKES 10 ROLLS

In the *bacari* these small rolls are often stuffed to the brim with thinly sliced prosciutto or speck and gorgonzola dolce. This recipe will also make a whole large flat focaccia that can then be cut into squares if you prefer. For a better flavour to the bread, make the dough the night before you need it and leave it in the bowl in the refrigerator. Remove the dough from the refrigerator the next day and shape into rolls straight away. It will take a little longer to rise from being stored in the cold. This will give higher acidity and larger holes in the *focaccine*. The rolls will be quite firm to bite and therefore good with fillings you can chew, such as sliced cured meat, bacon and grilled aubergine (eggplant). They are just irresistible while still warm.

Tip: This bread doesn't keep well but if you want to eat it the next day, allow it to cool, then wrap tightly in cling film (plastic wrap) to stop it drying out. It can also be frozen at this point. Any leftover rolls that have become dry can be split and toasted.

500 g (1 lb 2 oz/ 4 cups) strong white bread flour, plus extra for dusting

2 tbsp fine salt

1 sachet (7 g/¼ oz) dry yeast or 14 g (½ oz) fresh yeast

350 ml (12 fl oz/ 1½ cups) tepid water

4 tbsp extra virgin olive oil

Sea salt flakes to scatter over before baking

METHOD

Mix the flour and fine salt, and dried yeast if using, together in a large mixing bowl. If you are using fresh yeast, blend it into the water with your fingers until no lumps remain. Add the water to the flour and combine well using a plastic scraper or your hand to form a soft, pliable ball of dough. If it is too hard and dry, add a couple of tablespoons of water and only add more flour if the dough is really sticky; the dough should be only just dry enough to leave the bowl clean when you remove it, but not so dry that it is tough to work with.

Remove the dough from the bowl and place it on a lightly floured work surface. Knead the dough by pulling, stretching and folding it for around 10 minutes until it becomes more elastic and bounces back to the touch. Fold the edges of the dough underneath itself so that you have a smooth ball. Dust the bowl with 2 tablespoons of flour to prevent sticking and place the dough inside. Sprinkle a little more flour over the dough. Cover the bowl with cling film (plastic wrap) and leave in a warm, draught-free spot for about 1 hour or until it has doubled in volume.

Place the dough on a lightly floured work surface and, using your plastic scraper, cut it into 10 even-size pieces. I do this on a digital scale to make it easier. Weigh the whole ball of dough and divide by 10 so that you know the ideal weight of each roll. Make each one into a ball by tucking the edges underneath and then rolling between your hands. Put the balls onto a floured baking tray at least 4 cm (1¾ in) apart. Use your fingertips to make indentations in the tops of all the rolls, then drizzle a little oil over each one wiping it over the surface so that the they are covered in oil. This will prevent them getting a crust. Return the dough to its warm place to rise until it is about half as high again – 45 minutes to 1 hour. It should look puffy with little bubbles visible on the surface.

Preheat the oven to 220°C (425°F/ Gas 7). Sprinkle the dough balls with the sea salt flakes and bake in the oven for 15–17 minutes or until golden brown, then allow to cool in a basket or on a wire rack so that they cannot sweat underneath.

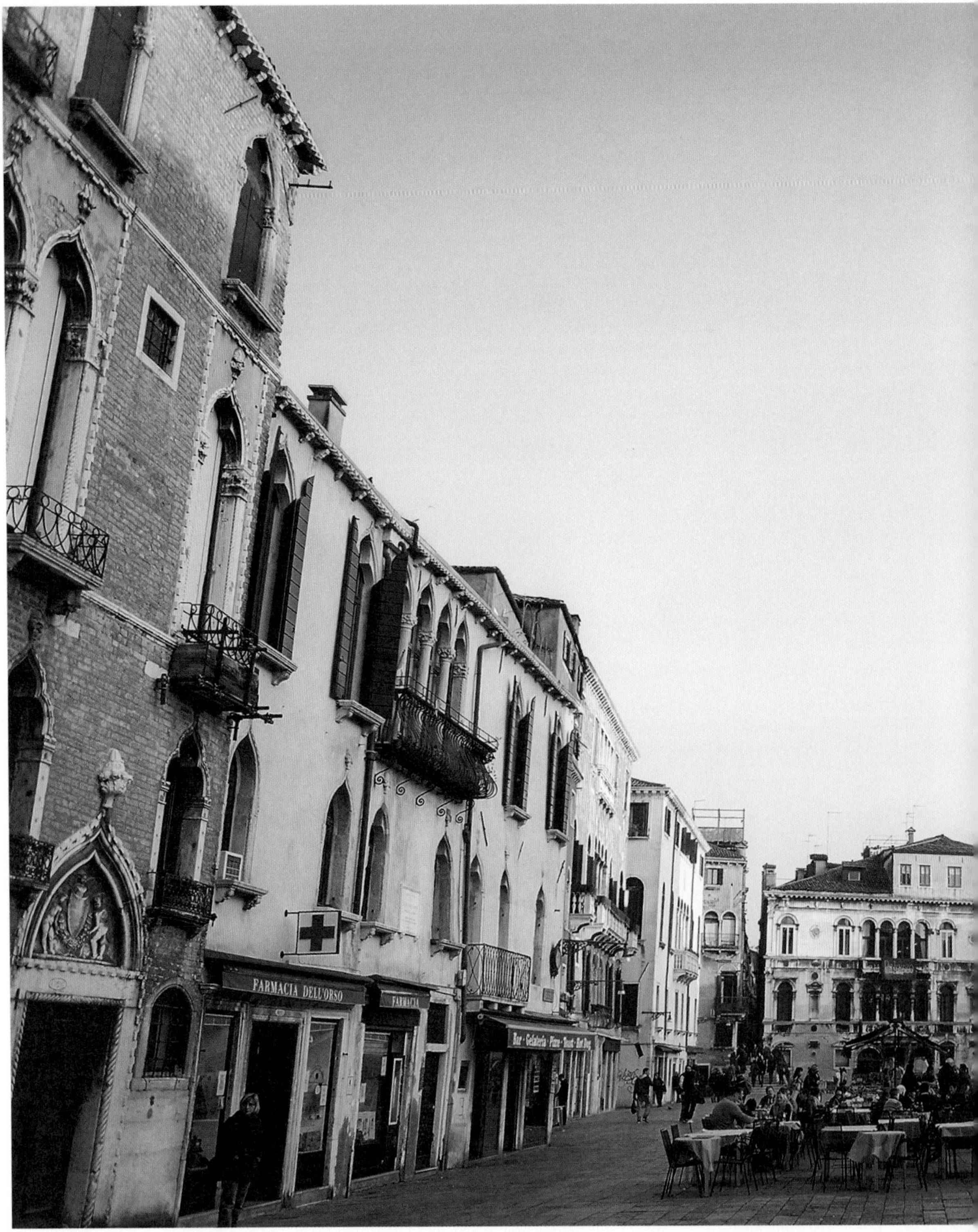
FARMACIA DELL'ORSO
FARMACIA

TORTE SALATE

Pies

In medieval and Renaissance Venice, little pies of mushroom, herbs and spinach were prepared by bakers as most people didn't have ovens at home. Large tarts and pies were commonplace in the grand palazzi and were prepared by cooks such as the Anonimo Veneziano. In his book *Libro per Cuoco* this unknown chef talks of a herb tart as well as many others made from lobster, broad (fava) beans, elderflower, mushrooms and more. He uses words to describe them like 'perfect', 'good' and 'optimal'.

BUONISSIMA TORTA DI CACCIAGIONE

Good Game Pie

SERVES 8–10

This is a great way of using leftover meat. I frequently do this with turkey at Christmas but hadn't thought of doing it with various game and duck. We have a ready supply of pheasants and pigeons near us and they are excellent in a pie such as this. Inspired by the rich game and mushroom pie in Francesco da Mosto's book *Francesco's Kitchen*, this is our version using pheasant and duck meat. If you prefer not to make the pastry, you can use ready-made shortcrust.

FOR THE PASTRY

200 g (7 oz/ 1⅔ cups) '00' or plain (all-purpose) flour, plus extra for dusting

Freshly ground black pepper

90 g (3¼ oz/ ⅓ cup) cold lard with a pinch of salt or salted butter, diced

4 tbsp cold white wine or water

50 g (1¾ oz) Parmesan, finely grated

FOR THE FILLING

500 g (1 lb 2 oz) chestnut or button mushrooms, sliced

3 sprigs of thyme

2 garlic cloves, lightly crushed

2 tbsp extra virgin olive oil

Salt and freshly ground black pepper

650 g (1 lb 7 oz) lean cooked meat such as game, duck or poultry (the sausages can be added too if following the cooking method for Pot Roast Game, see page 206)

200 ml (7 fl oz) strained cooking juices reserved from the casserole or stock used to cook the meat

100 g (3½ oz/ ½ cup) cooked risotto rice

50 g (1¾ oz) Parmesan, finely grated

2 tbsp parsley, finely chopped

3 eggs, beaten, plus 1 yolk to glaze

Pinch of ground saffron, to glaze

METHOD

Make the pastry following the instructions in the Fantastic Cheese, Spinach and Leek Pie recipe (see page 66).

While the pastry chills, preheat the oven to 180°C (350°F/Gas 4) and grease a 20 cm (8 in), 6 cm (2½ in) deep, loose-bottomed tin with butter. Fry the mushrooms with the thyme and garlic in the oil over a medium heat until soft, season well and remove from the heat. Discard the thyme and garlic. Remove the cooked meat from the bones and set aside. In a large saucepan, add the cooking juices and the cooked rice, and simmer for 5 minutes so that the rice absorbs the flavours of the juice. Pour the rice mixture into a large bowl to cool while you prepare the pastry case. Remove the pastry from the refrigerator and follow the instructions for rolling it out and lining the tin in the recipe on page 66.

Mix the meat, Parmesan, parsley, eggs and mushroom mixture into the rice mixture and pour into the lined tin. Don't worry if it is slightly proud of the tin. Roll out the lid and seal the edges using a fork or however you prefer. Poke a few holes in the lid with the tip of a small knife to allow the steam to escape. Brush with the beaten egg yolk and saffron to glaze. Cook for 45 minutes to 1 hour or until the pastry is browned and pulling away from the sides of the tin. Serve with salad and Perfect and Quick Pomegranate and Ginger Sauce (see page 208).

TORTA SALATA FANTASTICA CON FORMAGGIO, SPINACI E PORRI

Fantastic Cheese, Spinach and Leek Pie

SERVES 4

From the Anonimo Veneziano's recipe, we have made a sumptuous pie that is as delicious to eat as it is impressive to look at. If you can't find all the cheeses, just use a good local one with a medium strength. The trick to making good pastry is to keep everything very cold and use as little water as possible. Shop-bought sheets of shortcrust pastry are fine alternatives.

METHOD

To make the pastry, sift the flour into a mixing bowl and add the pepper. Using your fingers, rub in the lard and salt, or butter if using, until the mixture resembles fine breadcrumbs. Add the wine or water and bring the crumbs into a ball. (This can also be done in a food processor.) Knead briefly on a lightly floured work surface until you have a smooth dough. Wrap in plastic wrap and chill in the refrigerator for 20 minutes or overnight. (If you do leave it longer than 20 minutes, allow to soften a little at room temperature before rolling.)

Meanwhile, fry the leeks over a low heat in the oil and butter for around 15 minutes or until translucent. Steam or boil the spinach until tender, drain well and when cool squeeze dry with your hands. Chop finely or blitz in a food processor. Preheat the oven to 180°C (350°F/Gas 4) and grease a 20 cm (8 in), 6 cm (2½ in) deep, loose-bottomed tin with butter. Remove the leeks from the heat and drain them in a sieve over a bowl.

Flour the work surface and roll out the pastry to around 5 mm (¼ in) thick. Line the tin with the pastry by gathering it and pushing it out to the edges of the tin, and allowing it to flop over the top. Trim the excess pastry to 2 cm (¾ in) hanging over the tin, wrap it in plastic wrap and reserve for the lid. Chill the lined tin and the extra pastry again while you make up the fillings.

Combine the fontina or asiago with 2 beaten eggs in a bowl, season and set aside. In a separate bowl, mix the spinach, nutmeg and 2 beaten eggs together with the half the Parmesan. Season and set aside. Remove the lined tin from the refrigerator and cover the base with a layer of half of the leeks. Pour over the fontina mixture. Top this with the spinach mixture, flattening it down with a spatula. Beat the remaining

2 eggs with the remaining Parmesan and pour over the spinach. Finish with the remaining leeks.

Roll out the extra pastry to around 5 mm (¼ in) thick for the lid and lay over the top of the pie. I like to cut the lid so that it fits inside the rim and then I fold the edges of the casing pastry over it. If you find this difficult, simply use a fork to push the lid onto the casing, leaving little indentations around the edge. Poke a few holes in the lid with the tip of a small knife to allow the steam to escape. Beat 1 egg yolk with the pinch of saffron, if using, and brush over the pie. Decorate with shapers of left-over pastry by sticking them down with the glaze. Cook in the oven for 45 minutes or until the pastry is golden brown and pulling away from the edges of the tin. Take out and set aside to cool for at least 20 minutes before removing the tin from the pie and serving. Best served at room temperature with a light salad.

FOR THE PASTRY

200 g (7 oz/
1⅔ cups) '00' or
plain (all-purpose)
flour, plus extra
for dusting

Freshly ground
black pepper

90 g (3¼ oz/
⅓ cup) cold lard
with a pinch of
salt or salted
butter, diced

4 tbsp cold white
wine or water

50 g (1¾ oz)
Parmesan,
finely grated

1 egg yolk, to glaze

Pinch of ground
saffron, to glaze
(optional)

FOR THE FILLING

400 g (14 oz)
leeks, tough
dark green parts
discarded or
used for stock,
finely chopped

2 tbsp extra
virgin olive oil

25 g (1 oz/2 tbsp)
butter, plus extra
for greasing

375 g (13 oz)
spinach leaves,
washed and
stalks discarded

200 g (7 oz)
fontina, or asiago,
finely grated

6 eggs

Salt and freshly
ground black
pepper

¼ tsp nutmeg,
finely grated

100 g (3½ oz)
Parmesan or
grana padano,
finely grated

TORTA SALATA CON CARCIOFI E PARMIGIANO

Artichoke and Parmesan Pie

SERVES 6–8

In the fascinating Venetian cookery book *A Tola Co I Nostri Veci* by Mariù Salvatori de Zuliani, artichokes with a crust of white wine is mentioned. It refers to the recipe as antique but this tart is still seen in many places in Venice today. You can make it with fresh artichokes, but I prefer it with good-quality marinated artichokes in oil (see page 162).

1 quantity of pastry (see pages 66–67) or use two 215 g (7¹/₂ oz) sheets of ready-made puff pastry

METHOD

Make the pastry following the instructions in the Fantastic Cheese, Spinach and Leek Pie recipe (see page 66).

While the pastry is chilling, make the béchamel by heating the milk in a saucepan over a medium heat with the bay leaf, nutmeg and seasoning. Melt the butter in a separate larger saucepan over a medium heat, mix in the flour to make a roux and let it bubble for a few minutes. Remove the bay leaf from the milk, then pour it into the roux and whisk together over the heat until it thickens. Remove from the heat and set aside to cool for a few minutes. Stir in the artichokes, Parmesan and beaten eggs.

Preheat the oven to 180°C (350°F/ Gas 4) and grease a 24 cm (9½ in), 2.5 cm (1 in) deep loose-bottomed fluted tart tin. Remove the pastry from the refrigerator, put it onto a floured work surface and roll it out

to around 5 mm (¼ in) thick. Line the tin with the pastry, pressing lightly into the fluted sides, and cut off the extra pastry hanging over the sides. Fill with the artichoke and béchamel mixture. Roll out the remaining pastry to make a lid and use a rolling pin or a fork to seal the pastry together and cut off the excess. Beat the egg yolk with the pinch of saffron to make a glaze and brush the pie with it. Decorate with cut out shapes from any leftover pastry and prick the top in a few places with a small sharp knife to allow the steam to escape.

Bake in the oven for 30–40 minutes or until golden brown and the pastry has shrunk away slightly at the edges. Leave to cool slightly before removing from the tin. Serve with a simple dressed salad. This tart will reheat successfully in the oven loosely covered with foil.

FOR THE BÉCHAMEL

500 ml (17 fl oz / generous 2 cups) milk

1 bay leaf

¼ teaspoon freshly grated nutmeg

Salt and freshly ground black pepper

50 g (1¾ oz/ ½ stick) salted butter, plus extra for greasing

30 g (1 oz/¼ cup) '00' or plain (all-purpose) flour

FOR THE FILLING

450 g (1 lb) marinated artichokes in oil (shop-bought or homemade, see page 162), drained and cut into halves

50 g (1¾ oz) Parmesan, finely grated

3 eggs, beaten, plus 1 yolk to glaze

Pinch of ground saffron, to glaze

STRUDEL DI PORCINI E PECORINO

Porcini and Pecorino Strudels

SERVES 6

On a sunny October day we marvelled at an array of mushrooms spread out in autumnal glory at the Rialto market. The recognisable porcini were next to the chanterelles, known locally as *finferli*, and chiodini, the ones that look like little nails. Later for lunch at L'Osteria di Santa Marina we had a filo pastry bundle filled with the fresh porcini mushrooms layered with local asiago cheese. If you can't find asiago use pecorino, firm goat's cheese or brie.

TO COOK THE MUSHROOMS

Soak the porcini in a bowl of tepid water for at least 20 minutes. Strain off the water and discard, then squeeze out any excess water and chop them roughly. Warm the olive oil in a pan, add the chestnut mushrooms, garlic and herbs. Season and sauté over a high heat, tossing frequently for 10 minutes until the mushrooms have softened and browned. Add the porcini to the pan and fry for 2 more minutes. Take off the heat and tip the mushroom mixture into a large bowl or plate to cool to room temperature. Remove and discard the garlic and herbs.

TO MAKE THE PEPPER PURÉE

Cook the peppers whole on a baking tray with no oil or seasoning for 45 minutes until dark brown patches appear on the skin. Remove them from the oven and tip into a large bowl and cover with cling film (plastic wrap), or put them into a clean plastic bag, to sweat them. When cool enough to touch, peel and discard the skin from the peppers, cut them open, discard the stalk, seeds and pith and chop roughly.

Sweat the shallot in the oil in a large saucepan over a low heat until translucent. Add the peppers and stir. Add the rice and a ladle of vegetable stock and continue to cook over a medium heat, stirring frequently. Add the remaining stock a ladleful at a time, like a risotto, until most the stock has been absorbed and the rice is cooked; this should take around 25–30 minutes. Take off the heat, allow the mixture to cool slightly and then purée with a stick blender or food processor. Season to taste.

FOR THE MUSHROOM FILLING

20 g (¾ oz/1 cup) dried porcini

2 tbsp extra virgin olive oil

500 g (1 lb 2 oz) chestnut or other flavourful mushrooms, sliced 5 mm (¼ in) thick

1 large garlic clove, lightly crushed

3 sprigs of thyme

1 long sprig of rosemary

Salt and freshly ground black pepper

FOR THE PEPPER PURÉE

2 red (bell) peppers

1 shallot or small white onion, finely chopped

2 tbsp extra virgin olive oil

30 g (1 oz) arborio or other risotto or pudding rice

200 ml (7 fl oz/ scant 1 cup) vegetable stock

Salt and freshly ground black pepper

FOR THE STRUDELS

500 g (1 lb 2 oz) pack of filo pastry

100 g (3½ oz/ scant ½ cup) salted butter, melted for brushing the pastry

175g (6 oz) asiago, grated

Extra virgin olive oil, to serve

TO MAKE THE STRUDELS

Preheat the oven to 180°C (350°F/ Gas 4) and grease six 8 cm (3¼ in) deep and 4 cm (1½ in) wide ramekins or dariole moulds with melted butter. Cut 9 sheets of filo in half to make 18 squares. Lay one square out on a clean, dry work surface and brush with plenty of melted butter. Lay another square on top, brush with more butter, then add a final square so you have 3 layers of pastry. Now gather the edges together and push the pastry gently into a mould. Spoon in one-sixth of the mushroom mixture and then put one-sixth of the cheese on top. Pinch the filo sheets together so that it looks like a drawstring bag. Gently brush with more butter. Repeat for the remaining 5 moulds.

Cook in the oven for 20 minutes or until the parcels are golden brown and crisp. Heat the pepper purée; it may have thickened up as it contains rice, so add a little hot water to obtain a sauce consistency if necessary. Pour a circle or a line of it onto a warmed plate and carefully turn out the strudels from the moulds onto the sauce. Drizzle around some olive oil and serve.

At the Pasta Bar

Marco Polo is one of Venice's most famous characters, and I would love to credit him with bringing pasta from China to Italy but, as we now know from many sources, although he ate various forms of Asian noodles, these actually existed in Italy from at least as early as 1279, sixteen years before Marco Polo returned home. A legal document dated to this time, found in the possession of a Genovese soldier, mentioned '*una bariscella plena de macaronis*' – a basketful of macaroni.

Ravioli was a favourite in medieval cooking, often containing herbs and spices, mixed with cheese and eggs, then cooked in broth, and finished with more spices and sometimes sugar. Lasagne too would be coated with sugar and spice.

This sweetness carries through into Venetian gnocchi, made with pumpkin, which provides the perfect foil for a rich Lamb Ragù with Spices (see page 107) or a simple dressing of butter and sage.

Dried Pasta

Dried pasta is never judged as second rate to fresh pasta by Italians – it is simply more suited to certain sauces. Fresh pasta is more absorbent than dried, so it will drink a watery sauce such as seafood and become soft. Always pour just-drained hot pasta into a sauce and toss it well to make sure it is well coated before serving. The various shapes should be picked to complement the sauce; think of how tubes of penne hold little pieces of meat from the ragù or spaghetti becomes coated by a creamy sauce such as the sardines recipe below.

BIGOLI IN SALSA

Pasta with Sardines and Onions

SERVES 4 AS A MAIN OR 6 AS A STARTER

This is an unbelievably tasty dish made from just three main ingredients. The softened onions and fish form a creamy sauce to coat the pasta, which is incredibly moreish. This dish was typically eaten in Venetian households on Fridays during Lent, as in the past meat was banned. It is popular at all times now and also forms part of a grand fish feast on Christmas Eve in many homes. Use anchovies if you can't find sardines.

METHOD

Heat the oil in a large saucepan, add the onions and bay leaf, if using, and turn the heat to low. Cook slowly for around 15 minutes until soft, shaking and stirring the pan frequently with a wooden spoon. Rinse the fish in cold water if they are in salt; if they are in oil, don't worry. Bring to the boil a large pot of well-salted water, add the pasta and cook for 8–10 minutes or until al dente. Meanwhile, put the sardines in with the onions and break up the fish with a wooden spoon until they blend with the onions. Add the white wine to the fish and onions and allow the alcohol to evaporate for a couple of minutes. Season with pepper and taste, only add salt if necessary. Take a couple of ladlefuls of the water from the pot of pasta and reserve in a jug. Drain the pasta and add to the fish mixture with a little of the cooking water as necessary to create a sauce. Toss through and serve with a sprinkling of parsley if using.

A note on Parmesan: I have made Venetians gasp in horror as they rarely put fish and cheese together but a sprinkling of finely grated Parmesan is gorgeous on this dish.

4 tbsp extra virgin olive oil

2 large brown onions, finely chopped

1 small bay leaf (optional)

360 g (12½ oz) bigoli or spaghetti

240 g (8½ oz) tinned salted sardines or 60 g (2 oz) tinned anchovy fillets, net weight, in salt or oil

4 tbsp white wine

Salt and freshly ground black pepper

Handful of parsley, finely chopped, to serve (optional)

SPAGHETTI DI FARRO CON FUNGHI E CREMA DI PARMIGIANO

Spelt Spaghetti with Wild Mushrooms and Parmesan Cream

SERVES 4

Paolo Lazzari, who runs a restaurant called Vini da Gigio, loves his food and is justly proud of his wine list. He runs the restaurant with his sister, Laura, and chef Davide. They took it on from their late parents to keep on the family tradition. Paolo is wheat intolerant so many of the dishes are low in gluten. Yet he is able to eat spelt (an ancient wheat). We tried his spelt pasta made with chanterelles and a cream of Parmesan made from the 24-month old variety, which is crumbly, dry and full of intense flavour. I really like this cheese cream and in fact it is a useful sauce for all sorts of dishes. A Venetian luxury would be to top with some shaved black truffle.

METHOD

Put the spaghetti into a large pan of fiercely boiling well-salted water and stir through. Cook according to the packet instructions. Heat the oil in a frying pan over a high heat, add the garlic, rosemary and 4 sprigs of the thyme and cook for 2 minutes. If using the porcini, take them out of the water when soft and slice. Add all the mushrooms to the pan and fry them for 5–7 minutes until cooked through and the water has evaporated from them. Remove the pan from the heat and discard the sprigs of rosemary and thyme.

To make the Parmesan cream, melt the Parmesan into the cream in a small pan and keep over a very low heat.

Drain the pasta as soon as it is ready and tip it into the mushroom mixture, allowing a little of the cooking water to drip into the sauce to loosen it. Toss through and serve in warm bowls drizzled with the cheese cream, a swirl of extra virgin olive oil and the rest of the thyme leaves pulled from the stems.

320 g (11¼ oz) dried spelt, wholewheat or white spaghetti

5 tbsp olive oil

2 garlic cloves, peeled and lightly crushed

1 sprig of rosemary

5 sprigs of thyme

250 g (9 oz) chestnut or wild mushrooms, such as chanterelles, sliced

10 g (½ oz) dried porcini soaked in 100 ml (3½ fl oz/ scant ½ cup) water for 15 minutes (optional)

Extra virgin olive oil, to serve

FOR THE PARMESAN CREAM

50 g (1¾ oz) Parmesan, finely grated

100 ml (3¹/₂ fl oz/ scant ½ cup) double (heavy) cream

LINGUINE AL NERO DI SEPPIA CON GRANCHIO

Black Linguine with Crab

SERVES 4 AS A MAIN OR 6 AS A STARTER

Huge spider crabs are eaten as crab salad or tossed with pasta and often served in their shells. These crabs can also be found off UK shores but we don't have a history of eating them, so they are sold abroad, which is a huge shame. Their legs have an enormous amount of white, sweet meat in them. We love the crab with fresh white tagliolini served at the restaurant Antiche Carampane. Fresh pasta this thin is hard to cook perfectly, so we have given the option for using dried black or white pasta. The Venetians are not big on chilli, so add or leave out as you please.

Depending on whether you buy cooked crabs, their size and sex, or use pots of crabmeat, you will have differing amounts of white and brown meat. Always use more white crabmeat at the end of cooking and the stronger tasting brown crabmeat in smaller amounts at the beginning. If there is red coral in the crabs, add a little of this at the end for decoration. Most Venetian kitchens have at least three types of peppercorns; my favourite with this dish is a little crushed Sichuan at the end. As chilli strength varies from chilli to chilli, either add a little or a whole one. You have to be brave and taste to know!

4 tbsp extra virgin olive oil, plus extra to serve

2 shallots or 1 medium white onion, finely chopped

1 garlic clove, finely chopped

½–1 red fresh or dried chilli, finely chopped, to taste

2 crabs, cooked, or 100 g (3½ oz) brown crabmeat and 300 g (10½ oz) white crabmeat

100 ml (3½ fl oz/ scant ½ cup) Prosecco or white wine

Salt and freshly ground black or Sichuan pepper

1 quantity of fresh black or white tagliolini (see page 85) or 320 g (11¼ oz) dried black or white linguine

2 tbsps of parsley, finely chopped, leaves and stalks

METHOD

Bring a large saucepan of well-salted water to the boil. Heat the oil in a large frying pan and fry the shallots and garlic over a low heat until softened. Add the chilli and brown crabmeat and stir through. Turn up the heat and pour in the Prosecco, allow it to evaporate until the strong smell of alcohol has gone. Taste and season the sauce. Remove from the heat and set aside. Cook the pasta until just al dente. Take a few tablespoons of water from the pasta saucepan and add it to the frying pan. Drain the pasta and put this in too. Add the white crabmeat and parsley and toss or stir through briefly. Taste once more and season further if necessary. Drizzle with your finest olive oil and serve.

Spaghetti with Prawns and Tomato

SERVES 4 AS A MAIN OR 6 AS A STARTER

The wonderful chef Ada Catto worked at Ca' D'Oro – known locally as Alla Vedova, meaning the Widow's Place – for 30 years, where this dish was served in multitude every day. Ada uses chilli to give it a kick of spice, and other Venetians have told me they use paprika to give it a sweet spicy flavour. I make this dish spicy, so if you prefer it milder, then reduce the amount of chilli to suit your taste. Do taste the chilli before adding it to the dish as they vary in strength. Ada also recommended using good homemade tomato passata, but failing that use Italian tinned tomatoes and tomato purée (tomato paste). If you can find them use prawns (shrimp) with their heads still on, as that is where the flavour lies. If you can't find them, to get a stronger flavour of shellfish add 100 ml (3½ fl oz/scant ½ cup) of Seafood Stock (bouillon) (see page 117) with the tomatoes.

500 g (1 lb 2 oz) raw prawns (shrimp), shells and heads on if possible

Salt and freshly ground black pepper

50 g (1¾ oz/ ½ cup) '00' or plain (all-purpose) flour

2 garlic cloves, whole, peeled and lightly crushed

5 tbsp extra virgin olive oil

2 tbsp cognac

400 g (14 oz/ 1½ cups) tomato passata or tinned Italian whole plum tomatoes puréed in a blender

1 tbsp tomato purée (tomato paste)

½–1 red fresh or dried chilli, finely chopped, to taste, or 2 tbsp hot paprika

350 g (12 oz) spaghetti

Handful of parsley, finely chopped, to serve

METHOD

Remove the shells and tails from the prawns, leaving the heads attached to the body. Make a shallow cut down the length of the back of the body and remove the black vein. Put them into a mixing bowl and season, then add the flour and toss with your hands to coat the prawns. Fry the garlic in a large frying pan in the oil for 1 minute over a medium heat. Take the prawns from the flour, shaking off any excess, and add to the pan. Very briefly fry the prawns until they are pink and the flour has slightly browned. Add the cognac, shake the pan and when the strong smell of alcohol has dissipated, remove them from the pan with a slotted spoon. Set aside in a bowl. Leave the garlic in the pan and add the chilli, fry for 1 minute. Add the tomatoes and tomato purée, and leave it to cook, stirring every now and again, for 15–20 minutes over a low heat so it is just bubbling.

Bring a large pot of well-salted water to the boil and cook the spaghetti for 8–10 minutes or until al dente. Halfway through, put the prawns into the tomato sauce along with any juices in the bowl. Taste the sauce and season as necessary. Drain the pasta and add to the tomato sauce and toss or stir through the sauce. Divide among 4–6 warm bowls and scatter over the parsley to serve.

LINGUINE AI FRUTTI DI MARE

Linguine with Seafood

SERVES 4

This delicious dish is best cooked with really fresh shellfish, as the seawater trapped inside the shells is what makes it taste so good. Whole raw king prawns (jumbo shrimp) are also necessary for a great flavour. Most supermarkets tend to sell them already peeled with the heads and tails removed, but the heads contain the most flavour, so buy them whole if you can. At the restaurant Gatto Nero on Burano, an island in the Venetian Lagoon, they have a little trick of putting some grated Parmesan in the bottom of the bowl before putting the seafood linguine on top. Usually Italians don't mix cheese and fish but in this case it was really good. They also use more shellfish than pasta. The seafood will cook quickly, so prepare everything you need, get the pasta cooking and finish off the sauce.

1 kg (2 lb 4 oz) mixed seafood, such as squid rings around 1 cm (½ in) thick, clams, queen scallops, mussels, raw whole king prawns (jumbo shrimp)

350 g (12 oz) linguine or spaghetti

4 tbsp extra virgin olive oil

1 garlic clove, finely chopped

½ red chilli, finely sliced

Handful of parsley, roughly chopped

50 ml (2 fl oz/ ¼ cup) white wine

12 cherry tomatoes, halved

Good pinch of salt

30 g (1 oz) Parmesan, finely grated

METHOD

Clean the shellfish, removing the beards from the mussels, and drop the clams from a height of around 15 cm (6 in) into a bowl one by one to check for sand – it will come out as they land if dropped from this height. Discard any that are broken or are open and don't close with a tap, as they are dead. Remove the tails and shells from the bodies of the prawns, leaving their heads on.

Bring a large saucepan of well-salted water to the boil and cook the pasta until it is only just al dente.

Heat the oil in a large frying pan with a lid, add the squid and fry for 2 minutes. Add the rest of the seafood, the garlic, chilli and parsley. Put the lid on the pan and continue to cook for around 4–5 minutes, shaking the pan frequently. When all the shellfish shells have opened, pour in the wine and let it reduce, uncovered, until the strong smell of alcohol has dissipated. Discard any unopened shellfish. Then add the cherry tomatoes and salt.

Drain the pasta and toss it into the sauce. Let it cook in the juices for a couple of minutes. Divide the Parmesan into the bottom of 4 warm shallow bowls and top with the seafood pasta.

PASTA FRESCA

Fresh Pasta

The standard recipe for fresh pasta calls for 1 egg to every 100 g (3½ oz/scant 1 cup) of '00' flour. However, as eggs differ in size, a little experience is required to judge whether you need a little more water to soften the dough or a little more flour to stop it sticking. You only want the dough dry enough for it not to be sticky.

BASIC RECIPE FOR FRESH PASTA

MAKES ENOUGH LONG PASTA FOR 4 AS A MAIN OR 6 AS A STARTER

200 g (7 oz/ 1⅔ cups) '00' flour, plus a little for dusting if necessary

2 large free-range eggs

METHOD

Pour the flour into a mixing bowl and make a well in the middle. Crack the eggs into the well. Using a table knife, gradually combine the flour into the eggs, starting with the flour around the eggs and working your way out. Keep mixing the egg and flour until they form clumps of dough.

Use the fingertips of one hand to incorporate any remaining flour, bringing everything together until you have a ball of dough. Try to squash all the crumbs of dough into the ball, but discard any that don't make it. Remove the dough from the bowl and place on a floured work surface. Knead the dough by flattening and folding it for around 5–7 minutes, adding a little more flour if it is very sticky. Do this until it stops sticking to the palm of your hand. The dough should form a soft but firm ball that bounces back to the touch when prodded. If the dough becomes really dry and has many cracks, add 1–2 drops of water – do this in a bowl or food processor to rescue it.

Leave the pasta to rest covered in cling film (plastic wrap) for 20 minutes or for up to a day in the refrigerator. It is now ready to go through a pasta machine or to be rolled by hand.

BLACK PASTA

Black pasta is made by adding the black ink from cuttlefish (sometimes also called squid ink) to eggs and flour when making the pasta dough. It does have a slight fishy flavour, so is only used for seafood pasta recipes. The ink can vary in strength, cheaper versions being weaker so you will need to use more.

METHOD

As a rough guide, 2 tablespoons of ink (bought online or at good delis) is enough to colour 200 g (7 oz/ 1⅔ cups) '00' flour if mixed with 1 whole egg and 1 egg yolk.

Whisk the ink and eggs together first before adding to the flour, following the instructions on how to make fresh pasta, left.

If it looks a little grey, simply add more ink; if it becomes too soft, add more flour to compensate.

Cut into tagliolini or tagliatelle using the cutter on a pasta machine.

STUFFED PASTA

Many Italians use a ravioli mould to make stuffed pasta. If you have one, follow the instructions in Rita's Ravioli (see page 90) or fill by hand following these instructions.

METHOD

After resting, roll out the pasta through a pasta maker using the thinnest setting, so the pasta is thin but not too breakable. You should be able to see your hand or the pattern of a tablecloth through it.

Lay a sheet of pasta around 40 cm (16 in) in length onto a floured work surface, keeping the top surface of the pasta flour-free. Dot heaped teaspoons, around 6–10 g (¼–½ oz) of your filling onto the sheet, 3–4 cm (1¼–1¾ in) apart to leave sufficient space to cut and seal the pasta.

Lay another longer sheet of pasta over the top and press around each pile of filling to squeeze the air out and seal the pasta together. Use a round cutter, the rim of a glass or a pasta wheel to cut around each piece. Lay the ravioli onto a semolina- or flour-covered tray and continue making them until you run out of stuffing. To cut out *mezzaluna* – semicircles – dot the filling along the centre of a single sheet of pasta and fold it over. Press down as before to expel the air and use a wine glass or round cutter to cut out semicircles of filled pasta.

Cooking and serving the pasta

Pasta should always be cooked in plenty of well-salted water. It should be as salty as the sea, so about 320 g (11¼ oz) pasta to 4 litres (136 fl oz/17 cups) of water and 20 g (¾ oz) salt.

- Don't add oil to the water; it's expensive and rises to the surface rather than coating the pasta.
- Don't rinse the pasta after cooking. It will wash the last of the starch from the pasta which helps the sauce to stick to it.
- Don't leave fresh stuffed pasta hanging around, the filling will start to moisten the pasta and it will stick to whatever it is sitting on. Cook and serve straight away or pre-cook as opposite.

- Pre-cooking pasta is a good idea if you are not going to eat it straight away. Blanch ravioli in boiling salted water for 3–4 minutes or tagliolini for 1 minute, then drain and put onto a tray generously coated in sunflower oil, mixing the pasta with the oil so that it doesn't stick to itself or the tray. Allow to cool to room temperature and store in the refrigerator or freezer until needed. To reheat, drop the pasta into well-salted boiling water and cook for 2 minutes for ravioli and just 30 seconds for tagliolini, or until cooked through.
- Don't serve salad with pasta, particularly if it is dressed, as it will interfere with the flavour of the dish; eat it before or after the pasta course.

RAVIOLI DI RITA

Rita's Ravioli

SERVES 12 (MAKES AROUND 80-90 RAVIOLI)

Rita is from Vicenza, a small town not far from Venice. She lives in the UK now but still cooks *alla vicentina* and she makes the most wonderful *tortelli in brodo* for her family at Christmas. Luckily I know her daughter-in-law, so once a year I eat her ravioli in chicken broth. Like a mother's hug, this food is about as comforting as you can get. It is cooked and prepared with love and ladled out to children and adults alike over northern Italy. This recipe makes a lot of pasta but it does freeze well, so we make enough to eat straight away and freeze the rest for another day. The chicken stock (bouillon) is best homemade (see page 116) and flavoured with Parmesan rinds, which gives it a moreish, umami hit.

2 quantities of fresh pasta (see page 84)

3 litres (102 fl oz/ 12¾ cups) fresh or bought chicken stock (bouillon) (see page 116)

FOR THE FILLING

50 g (1¾ oz/ ½ stick) salted butter

½ onion or 1 small shallot, finely chopped

2 garlic cloves, finely chopped

100 g (3½ oz) minced (ground) veal or chicken or turkey

100 g (3½ oz) minced (ground) pork

4 tbsp white wine

Handful of parsley, finely chopped

60 g (2 oz/ ¾ cup) fresh breadcrumbs (see page 24)

50 g (1¾ oz) Parmesan, finely grated, plus extra to serve

1 egg yolk

Freshly ground black pepper and sea salt

METHOD

Melt the butter in a frying pan over a medium heat, then add the onion. After a few minutes, add the garlic and continue to gently fry until the onion softens. Don't let it burn. Add the minced meats and brown, stirring frequently. Pour in the wine. Cover, reduce the heat and cook gently for around 20 minutes, keeping an eye on it so that it doesn't catch. When the meat is very tender, carefully pour the mixture into a food processor and blend into a smooth paste. Transfer the blended meat to a mixing bowl and stir in the parsley, breadcrumbs, Parmesan and egg yolk. Combine well and season to taste.

Roll out the pasta using a pasta maker set on the thinnest setting. Line a ravioli tray with a sheet of the pasta. Spoon a fat pea-size ball of filling into each indent and place another sheet of pasta over the top. With a rolling pin, roll the pasta to ensure that the 2 layers are sealed together. If the pasta has dried out a little while you were dividing out the stuffing, brush with a little water before laying over the top sheet to ensure a good seal. Turn out onto greaseproof (wax) paper and repeat. The ravioli can be made in advance and frozen.

If you are using the homemade stock from page 116, leave the Parmesan rinds in. If using shop-bought stock, add 3 Parmesan rinds to it to give it the depth of flavour we need. Bring the chicken stock to a simmer in a large saucepan and season to taste. Add the ravioli and cook for around 12–14 minutes. This pasta is usually eaten soft rather than al dente. Serve with love and grated Parmesan.

TAGLIATELLE AL CACAO CON SALSA DI FORMAGGIO

Cocoa Tagliatelle with Cheese Sauce

SERVES 4 AS A MAIN OR 6 AS A STARTER

This pasta is wonderful with the Parmesan Cream from the Spelt Pasta with Wild Mushrooms.

METHOD

Make the Parmesan Cream from page 76. Follow the recipe for making fresh cocoa pasta (see page 93). Cut it into tagliatelle on the pasta machine or by hand. Cook and toss with the Parmesan Cream.

RAVIOLI AL CACAO RIPIENI DI GORGONZOLA E NOCI

Cocoa Ravioli stuffed with Gorgonzola and Walnuts

SERVES 6 (MAKES 30 RAVIOLI)

This recipe is from Ivan, the owner of Pastificio Serenissima in Castello. The cocoa gives the pasta a gorgeous nuttiness in flavour and a rich chocolate colour which contrasts brilliantly with the melting gorgonzola and crunchy walnuts inside. Try to find creamy gorgonzola dolce, which has a sweet, mellow flavour instead of the harsher crumbly gorgonzola piccante. Any leftover cocoa pasta can be rolled out again and cut into tagliatelle, which is lovely with the Parmesan Cream on page 76.

METHOD

Make the pasta by following the basic fresh pasta recipe on page 84, but mix the cocoa powder into the flour first and add in the extra egg yolk. You may need to add the water if the pasta is very dry, as the cocoa powder is very absorbent.

Combine all the ingredients for the filling in a bowl and season to taste.

Make the ravioli by hand following the instructions for making Rita's Ravioli on page 90. Bring to the boil a large saucepan of well-salted water and cook the ravioli for around 5 minutes or until al dente.

To make the sauce, heat the butter in a large frying pan with the rosemary for a couple of minutes. Add a squeeze of lemon juice and shake the pan to blend it together. Discard the sprig of rosemary. Drain the pasta and add it to the pan. Shake the pan to coat the ravioli in sauce. Serve on warm plates or shallow bowls with Parmesan.

FOR THE PASTA

200 g (7 oz/ 1⅔ cups) '00' flour

2 whole eggs, plus 1 egg yolk

15 g (½ oz/2 tbsp) cocoa powder

1 tbsp water, if necessary

FOR THE FILLING

50 g (1¾ oz/ ½ cup) walnuts, finely chopped

200 g (7 oz) gorgonzola dolce

100 g (3½ oz/ ⅓ cup) ricotta

30 g (1 oz) Parmesan, finely grated

Salt and freshly ground black pepper

FOR THE SAUCE

75 g (2½ oz/ generous ½ cup) salted butter

1 sprig of rosemary

Squeeze of lemon juice

30 g (1 oz) pecorino or Parmesan, finely grated, to serve

RAFFIOLI DE HERBE

Cheese-filled Ravioli in Saffron and Herb Sauce

SERVES 4 AS A MAIN OR 6 AS A STARTER

This is a stunning dish to serve. The plump ravioli are filled with three kinds of cheese, bathed in glorious saffron sauce and decorated with aromatic leaves. The recipe is an adaption of the original by the Anonimo Veneziano, created by Sergio and Mario at the restaurant Bistrot de Venise where it forms part of their historical Venetian menu.

1 quantity of fresh pasta (see page 84)

FOR THE FILLING

200 ml (7 fl oz/ scant 1 cup) milk

50 g (1¾ oz/scant ½ cup) '00' flour

100 g (3½ oz) cheese, such as pecorino, fontina or asiago

60 g (2 oz) soft goat's cheese

50 g (1¾ oz) Parmesan or grana padano, finely grated

Salt and freshly ground black pepper

2 egg yolks

FOR THE SAUCE

50 g (1¾ oz/ ½ stick) salted butter

2 tbsp extra virgin olive oil

2 celery stalks with leaves, chopped

2 leeks, chopped

1 litre (34 fl oz/ 4½ cups) chicken stock

1 heaped tsp grated fresh ginger

½ tsp saffron

Salt and freshly ground black pepper

TO SERVE

50 g (1¾ oz/ ½ stick) salted butter

Large handful of aromatic leaves such as rosemary, thyme, sage or marjoram

30 g (1 oz) toasted flaked (slivered) almonds

30 g (1 oz) smoked cheese, such as ricotta, scamorza or smoked Cheddar, coarsely grated

METHOD

For the filling, heat the milk in a medium saucepan over a medium heat, whisk in the flour and continue whisking over the heat until thick and any lumps have disappeared. Turn the heat to low and add the cheeses, season and whisk through. Take the pan off the heat and whisk in the egg yolks. Taste and adjust the seasoning as necessary, then allow to cool to room temperature.

Prepare and fill the pasta according to the instructions on page 93, using 10 g (½ oz) of filling per raviolo and using a 6 cm (2½ in) cutter or wine glass to cut the pasta.

To make the sauce, in a large frying pan, heat the butter and oil and fry the celery and leeks over a medium heat until softened. Add the stock, ginger, saffron and seasoning, turn up the heat and bring to the boil.

Reduce the heat and simmer gently for 15 minutes. Taste and adjust the seasoning as necessary. Purée the sauce in a blender and set aside.

To assemble the dish, melt the butter in a frying pan and add the herbs. Fry them for around 2 minutes, take off the heat and set aside. Bring a large saucepan of well-salted water to the boil and cook the ravioli for around 5 minutes or until al dente. Reheat the sauce in a large saucepan and add the drained pasta to it. Arrange the ravioli on each plate with a little of the sauce poured over the top. Drizzle the herby butter around the plate. Scatter over the flaked almonds and grated cheese, then stand back and admire your work!

CASUNZIEI AMPEZZANI

Half Moons of Pasta Filled with Beetroot in Poppy Seed Butter

SERVES 4

This is a traditional dish of the skiing area of Cortina in the Dolomites. As cooks and chefs have moved from different areas to Venice, they have brought their traditions with them. We love this pretty dish of half-moon shaped pasta filled with pink beetroot stuffing and served with poppy seeds and butter. They should be served just coated in butter rather than enjoying a swim in it.

1½ quantity
of fresh pasta
(see page 84)

FOR THE FILLING

250 g (9 oz)
cooked beetroot

100 g (3½ oz)
cooked potato

100 g (3½ oz/
1¼ cups) fresh
breadcrumbs
(see page 24)

2 egg yolks

¼ tsp ground
nutmeg

½ tsp fine salt

Freshly ground
black pepper

FOR THE SAUCE

100 g (3½ oz/
scant ½ cup)
salted butter

¼ tsp ground
cinnamon

TO SERVE

1–2 tsp poppy
seeds

30 g (1 oz)
Parmesan or
smoked cheese,
shaved

METHOD

To make the filling, blend the beetroot and potato in a food processor, or mash by hand, until smooth. Transfer to a mixing bowl and stir in the breadcrumbs, egg yolks, nutmeg, salt and season with pepper to taste.

Prepare and stuff the pasta following the instructions for Rita's Ravioli (see page 90) using a 6 cm (2½ in) round cutter or large wine glass to cut out the half-moon shapes.

Melt the butter with the cinnamon in a large saucepan, then turn off the heat so you don't burn the butter. Bring a large saucepan of well-salted water to the boil and cook the half moons for 5–6 minutes until al dente. Drain the pasta and add to the butter in the pan. Shake the pan so that the *mezzaluna* become coated in butter. Serve in warm shallow bowls and scatter with poppy seeds and Parmesan.

GNOCCHI DI PATATE

Potato Gnocchi

SERVES 8

Gnocchi are best made with potatoes that are neither too fluffy nor too smooth, and the Italians say they should be boiled in their skins so that the water doesn't saturate the potatoes. The secret to light gnocchi is to trap as much air inside as you can by pushing the cooked potatoes through a sieve, a *passatutto* (food mill) or a ricer. Freezing gnocchi before they are cooked can give an even better result than cooking from fresh, as they tend to hold their shape better. A Venetian pasta maker told me that his mother would fry any leftover cooked gnocchi for breakfast with butter, and then dust them with sugar and cinnamon.

1 kg (2 lb 4 oz) potatoes (Désirée work well)

2 eggs, beaten

2 teaspoons fine salt

Freshly ground black pepper

300 g (10½ oz/ 2½ cups) '00' flour

METHOD

Bring a large pan of salted water to the boil and cook the potatoes in their skins until tender – this may take up to 1 hour, depending on their size. Drain and peel them while they are still hot, by holding them in one hand with a fork or a cloth and peeling the skin away with a knife in the other hand.

Pass the potatoes through a sieve, ricer or food mill into a large mixing bowl. Stir in the egg with a wooden spoon. Add the salt and a good twist of black pepper, then add half of the flour and combine. Pour the rest of the flour into a mound on the work surface, make a well in it and put the dough into the well. Use your hands to knead in the rest of the flour to form a firm but pliable dough.

Lightly flour a large board or section of your work surface next to where you are preparing the gnocchi. On a clean surface, roll the dough into long sausages around 2 cm (¾ in) wide. Cut the sausages into 2 cm (¾ in) lengths. Gently roll each piece into a ball between your palms. Use the side of your thumb to carefully roll the ball on a grater to make indentations and form a pattern, then place the gnocco onto your floured board. Repeat this for the rest of the dough. As you roll the gnocchi on the grater, a cavity will also from where your thumb was. This and the indentations will be perfect to collect the sauce.

Bring another large saucepan of well-salted water to the boil. Drop in the gnocchi. When they bob up to the surface they are done – this takes about 2–4 minutes. Drain well and toss into a sauce, such as the mushroom sauce or Parmesan Cream on page 76 or the butter and sage sauce from page 102, heated in a large frying pan.

If you plan to freeze your gnocchi before cooking, spread them out on a well-floured baking tray, making sure they don't touch each other, and put the tray in the freezer. When frozen (which takes around 3 hours), shake off any excess flour and transfer the gnocchi to a freezer bag to take up less space. Use within 3 months. To cook from frozen, allow an extra 1–2 minutes cooking time.

GNOCCHI RIPIENI DI ZUCCA

Pumpkin-stuffed Gnocchi

SERVES 6 AS A MAIN OR 8 AS A STARTER (MAKES 90–100 GNOCCHI)

Tucked away in the Castello area of Venice we saw an intriguing display of pasta and gnocchi in the window of Pastificio Serenissima. We went inside and met the owner Ivan and he showed us his speciality recipes. He had invented a potato gnocchi that was stuffed with pumpkin and cheese. Pumpkins are available all year round in the Veneto. The two main types are the smooth green zucca mantovana, which has bright orange flesh and is always available, and the seasonal zucca barucca with a knobbly, bumpy skin. Ivan told us to adjust the quantity of bread according to how much water there is in the pumpkin.

1 quantity of Potato Gnocchi (see page 101)

00 flour for dusting

FOR THE FILLING

300 g (10½ oz) peeled, seeded pumpkin, cut into approximately 5 cm (2 in) cubes

100 g (3½ oz) Parmesan, finely grated

1 egg, plus 1 egg yolk

150 g (5½ oz/ 2 cups) soft breadcrumbs (see page 24)

Grating of nutmeg

1 teaspoon salt

1 sprig of rosemary, finely chopped

FOR THE SAUCE

100 g (3½ oz/ scant ½ cup) salted butter

15–20 sage leaves

Freshly ground black pepper

50 g (1¾ oz) Parmesan, finely grated

METHOD

Preheat the oven to 180°C (350°F/ Gas 4). Put the pumpkin in a large baking tin, cover with foil and roast for 40 minutes. Remove the foil and roast for another 15 minutes or until soft. Make sure the pumpkin doesn't brown. Remove from the oven and allow to cool. Put the flesh into a food processor and blend or into a large mixing bowl and mash by hand. Add the rest of filling ingredients, stir to combine and set aside.

Make the potato gnocchi following the instructions on page 101. Instead of making sausage shapes, roll out the dough with a rolling pin into a rough rectangle 5 mm (¼ in) thick. Fill a piping bag with the filling mixture and 4 cm (1½ in) down from the top edge, pipe a 2 cm (¾ in) thick sausage of stuffing. Fold the top edge of the dough over the filling and seal it in by gently pressing down with your fingers. Cut the length of gnocchi away from the rectangle and cut into pieces around 2 cm (¾ in) wide and 4 cm (1½ in) long. Set aside on a clean tea towel (dish cloth). Repeat the piping, folding, sealing and cutting process down the rest of the rectangle.

Melt the butter with the sage leaves and black pepper in a large frying pan over a low heat. Bring a large saucepan of well-salted water to a gentle boil. Drop in the gnocchi. When they float up to the surface they are done – this takes about 2 minutes. Remove the gnocchi from the water with a slotted spoon and add them into the frying pan. Toss through and serve in warm bowls with Parmesan.

MACCHERONI DI ZUCCA CON RAGÙ D'AGNELLO SPEZIÀ

Pumpkin Gnocchi for Lamb Ragù with spices

SERVES 6–8

These were originally called *maccheroni* in the Veneto during the medieval period. They have continued to be made to this day, usually with the green fat pumpkins called mantovana. Mario, the chef at Bistrot de Venise, showed us a way to make these pumpkin gnocchi by pushing the mixture through a piping bag and snipping off pieces into boiling water with scissors. He serves them with the equally ancient recipe for Lamb Ragù with Spices (see page 107). We've used readily-available butternut squash instead of mantovana.

METHOD

Preheat the oven to 180°C (350°F/ Gas 4). Wash the butternut squash and cut into wedges around 5 cm (2 in) at the thickest part, leaving the skin on. Put the wedges into a baking tray and brush with the olive oil. Cook for 30–40 minutes until soft. Remove from the oven and leave to cool. Scoop the flesh off the skins into a food processor. Add the eggs, egg yolks, cheese, flour and seasoning, and blend until smooth.

Bring a large saucepan of well-salted water to the boil. Put the gnocchi mixture into a piping bag with a 2 cm (¾ in) nozzle. Over the pan of boiling water, push the mixture through the bag and snip off the first gnocchi at 2 cm (¾ in) so that it falls into the water. Work fast and continue until a third of the mixture is used. When the gnocchi come to the surface they are cooked. Scoop them out with a slotted spoon and put into a warm serving dish coated with some sunflower oil. Brush more oil over the gnocchi in the dish so they don't stick together. Repeat with the rest of the mixture in 2 more batches, each time coat the gnocchi in the dish with some sunflower oil. The gnocchi can be kept in the refrigerator or frozen like this, or used straight away. To serve with ragù (see page 107), heat the ragù in a large non-stick frying pan and then add the gnocchi. If the gnocchi have been stored in the refrigerator, reheat them by putting them in boiling salted water for 30 seconds, drain and add to the ragù.

1.6 kg (3 lb 8 oz) butternut squash, approximately 2 squashes

3 tbsp extra virgin olive oil

3 eggs, plus 2 egg yolks

100 g (3½ oz) Parmesan, grated

300 g (10½ oz/ 2½ cups) '00' flour

Salt and freshly ground black pepper

Sunflower oil

RAGÙ D'AGNELLO SPEZIATO

Lamb Ragù with Spices

SERVES 6–8

This medieval recipe is spiced with cinnamon and cloves. It has no tomatoes as in those days they had not yet been discovered. It is perfect served with the Pumpkin Gnocchi on page 104 but is equally delicious served with Potato Gnocchi (see page 101).

1.25 kg (2 lb 12 oz) lamb shoulder

4 tbsp extra virgin olive oil

200 g (7 oz) leeks, finely chopped

1 garlic clove, lightly crushed

7 cloves, ground

3 cm (1¼ in) cinnamon stick

Salt and freshly ground black pepper

200 ml (7 fl oz/ scant 1 cup) white wine

750 ml (25 fl oz/ 3 cups) beef stock (bouillon) *(chicken or vegetable would also work)*

Parmesan, finely grated, to serve

FOR THE BOUQUET GARNI

4 large sage leaves

5 short sprigs of thyme

1 long sprig of rosemary, cut into pieces

METHOD

Cut the lamb into 5 cm (2 in) cubes and set aside in a bowl in the refrigerator. Heat the oil in a large heavy-based saucepan and fry the leeks gently over a low heat for around 10 minutes. Add the garlic and continue to sweat for a further 5 minutes until the leeks are soft and translucent. Remove the lamb from the refrigerator and add to the pan. Stir through, then add cloves, cinnamon and seasoning. Cook the lamb over a medium heat for around 30 minutes, stirring frequently, until all the water from the meat has evaporated and the lamb is dry.

Meanwhile, make a bouquet garni by bundling the herbs together in the middle of a muslin cloth (cheesecloth), close it up to make a bag and secure with string. Add the wine, stock and bouquet garni to the pan and cook for around 1 hour or until the sauce has reduced by half and the lamb is soft. Taste and season further as necessary. Remove the cinnamon stick and bouquet garni. Toss with gnocchi and sprinkle with grated Parmesan.

Polenta

Polenta, made from ground cornmeal, is a big deal in the north of Italy and taken very seriously, each restaurant or household having their favourite way of cooking and serving it. In Venice you will see it in various guises; white, yellow, soft and set firm. Our friend Luca described the soft white polenta – which is served under *schie*, the local small prawns (shrimp), tossed with butter, garlic and parsley – as 'like eating a cloud'. Then you will see fine yellow polenta perhaps mixed with rosemary and set into squares that are topped with wild mushrooms. One of my favourites is polenta *grossa* or *grezzo*; bright yellow coarsely ground polenta mixed with Parmesan and served soft with a meat ragù or casserole.

Originally from Turkey it was introduced to the Italians to save them from famine after the plague struck. They loved it and ate loads of it, in fact so much so that they ate polenta and nothing else. Malnutrition followed and eating polenta was seen as the cause, so the authorities banned it. However, some years later when the famine returned, a clever doctor worked out it wasn't the polenta that made people malnourished but the restricted diet. People started eating polenta again as part of a balanced diet and life was good again. Polenta has been loved ever since and most Venetians will remember their mother or grandmother cooking it in a large copper pan, hot splashes hitting their arms. I think they form an emotional link with it from childhood, perhaps as we British do with our mother's mashed potato. Certainly no one made mash as well as my mother in my mind, from her choice of potato to the amount of butter and seasoning she added. The slow art of making polenta is no different.

White polenta, made from white corn, is typically used in Venice. It is usually made from the corn variety 'biancoperla' and finely ground, and it has a delicate flavour, so is traditionally favoured for seafood dishes characteristic of Venice. My favourite polenta dish was cooked at the restaurant Al Covo where we had white polenta with Parmesan, drizzled with Tuscan green olive oil and scattered with more Parmesan. This was a little amuse bouche served at every table as a welcome. It was sublime.

Yellow corn polenta can be fine and smooth or rough and gritty. It is more common on the mainland and better with meat dishes, especially when made from the corn variety 'marano' or 'maranello'. Any variety can be used as a flour to give a pleasant grainy texture to cakes and biscuits such as the Venetian Yellow Polenta Biscuits on page 235.

Giancarlo's father used to measure polenta with a *manciata*, which was a fistful of polenta that he let fall slowly from his hand held at head height. He added to boiling, salted water, whisking it in as it fell. To cook polenta in milk was considered wasteful in his day but actually we now recommend half milk and half water or vegetable stock (bouillon).

The quick-cooking polenta is used commonly in Venice and it is ready in just 5 minutes. There is a subtle difference in texture and flavour but I have to say only polenta aficionados would notice! If you do make it, follow the packet instructions.

Polenta

SERVES 6 (MAKES 24 SQUARES)

Both set and soft polenta is made in the same way but more water is added to the soft version. Sous chef Daniele Malagni gave us his tip of adding butter at the end, which helps keep it soft. Once set polenta has cooled, it becomes solid and can be cut into shapes and grilled or fried. It forms a good base for Cicchetti (see page 34) or cut into chips and deep-fried. The friendly chef Dimitri Gris at Il Covino told us that one day he accidentally dropped some chopped rosemary into his pot of yellow polenta. Just before the service, he had no time to make any more. His customers loved it and so he has been doing it ever since.

TO MAKE SET POLENTA

Bring the water to the boil in a large saucepan. From a height, slowly pour the polenta into the boiling water. Add the rosemary if using. Stir constantly for 5 minutes and then every 5 minutes for a further 35 minutes. Taste and add salt as necessary. Remove from the heat and stir in the cheese. Oil a shallow tin roughly 20 × 30 × 1.5 cm (8 × 12 × ¾ in) or a work surface and pour the polenta onto it. Spread a little oil on top and flatten it down with an oiled spatula to 2 cm (¾ in) thick, then leave to cool and set firm. Cut into twenty-four 5 cm (2 in) squares. The polenta can be dipped into plain (all-purpose) flour, shaking off any excess, and fried in sunflower oil in a frying pan over a medium-high heat or simply toasted under a grill until lightly browned.

TO MAKE SOFT POLENTA

Follow the recipe for set polenta but add a further 200 ml (7 fl oz/ scant 1 cup) water and stir in 100 g (3½ oz/scant ½ cup) butter at the end. This gives a rich flavour and a glossy finish.

TO MAKE BLACK POLENTA

Black polenta is made by adding cuttlefish ink (sometimes called squid ink) to the polenta as it is being cooked; add spoonfuls of ink until you have the right density of colour. The better quality of ink you buy (either online or from an Italian deli), the less ink you will need. It is available in jars or sachets.

1 litre (34 fl oz/ 4½ cups) water

150 g (5½ oz/1 cup) white fine or yellow polenta

Leaves from 1 sprig of rosemary, finely chopped (optional)

2 tsp fine salt

100 g (3½ oz) Parmesan, finely grated

Sunflower oil

Stocks, Rice, Beans and Soups

Don't throw anything away. Make stock (bouillon) using vegetable peelings, raw or cooked chicken carcasses or fish bones and prawn (shrimp) shells (freeze them for later use if necessary). If they are frozen, don't bother defrosting them, just add them to the pot. A good stock is essential, as we all know, to add flavour to soups, stews and above all risotto. The better the stock, the better the flavour of the final dish. Make stocks on Sundays or when you are at home and not rushing about. They need time to bubble away, making the house smell like a home. Reduce them to an intense concentration and freeze them in small batches ready to be defrosted and diluted with water as necessary.

BRODO DI VERDURE

Vegetable Stock

MAKES 2 LITRES (68 FL OZ/8½ CUPS)

Instead of whole vegetables, use the peelings from carrots, onions and leeks, parsley stalks and celery. As you create these trimmings over the period of a week or so, keep them in a plastic bag in the freezer, adding to the bag as you make more. Use these for a wonderful stock (bouillon) for free.

METHOD

Heat the oil in a large stockpot over a medium heat and add all the ingredients except the water. Fry them together for around 5 minutes and then add the water, increase the heat and bring to the boil. Reduce the heat and simmer gently for 1 hour. Remove from the heat and allow to cool. Strain the stock into a large jug or bowl and return the stock to the pan, discarding the vegetables. Use straight away, store in the refrigerator for up to 4 days or freeze for up to 3 months.

1 tbsp olive oil

1 large tomato, with a cross cut in the top

2 celery stalks and leaves, roughly chopped (or the equivalent in peelings)

1 carrot, roughly chopped (or the equivalent in peelings)

4 leeks, roughly chopped (or the equivalent in peelings)

2 onions, peeled and roughly chopped (or the equivalent in peelings)

Small handful of parsley stalks, chopped

Handful of flat-leaf parsley, chopped

2 bay leaves

1 sprig each of rosemary, thyme and sage

2 garlic cloves, lightly crushed

3 Parmesan rinds (around 200 g/ 7 oz – optional)

3 litres (102 fl oz/ 12¾ cups) hot water

BRODO DI POLLO DI RITA

Rita's Chicken Stock

MAKES 1–3 LITRES (34–102 FL OZ/4¼– 12¾ CUPS)

Our friend Rita from Vicenza, just south of Venice, makes her chicken stock (bouillon) from either a whole chicken or from carcasses. In Italy you can buy an old egg-laying bird with feet and head intact, which makes a really tasty stock. Somehow even our free-range birds that strut through life happily don't seem to have the flavour we seek. However, Rita's secret is to include at least two Parmesan rinds. This makes a huge difference. I really believe Parmesan is a natural flavour enhancer; it doesn't always make things taste cheesy but just brings out the other flavours in a dish.

METHOD

In a large stockpot, heat the oil over a medium heat and brown the chicken with the carrots, onion and celery, stirring frequently. When they start to stick to the bottom of the pan, add the water, parsley, Parmesan rinds, bay leaf and dried porcini, if using. Turn up the heat to bring to the boil, then reduce the heat and simmer for 3 hours. At this point the stock is ready for using and will give you around 3 litres (68 fl oz/12¾ cups). Simmer for longer if you want a more concentrated stock for freezing. Remove from the heat and strain into a large jug or bowl. Discard everything except the Parmesan rinds, which should be added back into the broth. Use straight away, store in the refrigerator for up to 4 days or freeze for up to 3 months.

3 tbsp extra virgin olive oil

1½–2 kg (3 lb 5 oz– 4 lb 6 oz) raw or cooked chicken bones or carcasses

2 carrots, roughly chopped

1 onion, roughly chopped

2 celery stalks and leaves, roughly chopped

5 litres (170 fl oz/ 20¼ cups) hot water

Small bunch of parsley tied with string

3 Parmesan rinds (around 200 g/7 oz)

1 bay leaf

5 g (¼ oz/¼ cup) dried porcini mushrooms (optional)

BRODO DI GAMBERI

Seafood Stock

MAKES 2 LITRES (68 FL OZ/8½ CUPS)

3 tbsp extra
virgin olive oil

1½ kg (3 lb 5 oz)
seafood shells

1 carrot, halved
lengthways

1 onion, quartered

100 ml (3½ fl oz/
scant ½ cup)
white wine

3 litres (102 fl oz/
12¾ cups)
hot water

In our house, anytime we cook shellfish, we keep and freeze the shells, including the heads. When we have enough, we make stock (bouillon), reduce it and freeze it again. Use shells from crabs, prawns (shrimp), crayfish, langoustine and lobsters.

METHOD

Heat the oil in a large stockpot over a medium heat and brown the shells with the carrot and onion. When they start to stick to the bottom of the pan, add the wine, increase the heat and let it reduce for 4–5 minutes. Bash the shells, particularly any prawn or lobster heads, with a wooden rolling pin to release the juices and break up the shells. Add the water, bring to the boil, reduce the heat and simmer for 1–1½ hours. Remove from the heat. Strain over a large jug or bowl, squeezing the juices from the shells by pressing down with the ladle. Discard the shells. Use the stock straight away, store in the refrigerator for up to 4 days or freeze for up to 3 months.

FUMETTO DI PESCE

Fish Stock

MAKES 2 LITRES (68 FL OZ/8½ CUPS)

1 kg (2 lb 4 oz)
white fish bones

1 celery stalk,
roughly chopped

1 celery heart,
roughly chopped

1 carrot, roughly
chopped

1 white onion,
halved

2 tbsp olive oil

10 black
peppercorns

2 tomatoes

2 bay leaves

Small bunch of
fresh parsley

3 litres (102 fl oz/
12¾ cups)
cold water

The spines from white fish such as sea bass and mullet are often unwanted by fishmongers, so if you ask them they will keep them for you. I freeze the bones of fish ready for when I need to make a fish stock (bouillon).

METHOD

Put all the ingredients into a large stockpot. Bring to the boil over a high heat, then reduce the heat and simmer for 30 minutes, skimming off the foam that floats on top regularly with a slotted spoon. Take off the heat and strain the stock into a large jug or bowl through a piece of muslin (cheesecloth) or a fine sieve. Discard the bones, then leave the stock to rest for 1 hour until the sediment has settled. Ladle off the stock into a clean jug or bowl, avoiding the sediment at the bottom. Discard the sediment. Use or store as for Seafood Stock above.

SOFFRITTO

Soffritto

A soffritto is a mixture of finely chopped vegetables that are fried slowly in extra virgin olive oil to give a wonderful base flavour to soups, ragù and stews. Sometimes garlic and herbs such as rosemary, bay and thyme are added.

METHOD

Make soffritto with 2 celery stalks, 1 large white onion and 2 medium carrots. Peel and finely chop the vegetables by hand or in a food processor and the soffritto is ready to use.

ZUPPA DI ZUCCA

Pumpkin Soup

SERVES 6–8

This soup was served to us at the restaurant of the same name, La Zucca, where they serve mainly vegetarian food and primarily dishes made with pumpkin. This soup is loosely based on their recipe. Use the best quality pumpkin you can find. In Venice, they mainly use the mantovana pumpkin variety, which is squat, large and pale green. They don't purée it like you see in most pumpkin soup recipes; the hearty chunks of vegetables make it all the more interesting. Remember to save your peelings for a vegetable stock.

500 g (1 lb 2 oz) pumpkin (around ½ butternut squash), peeled

1 carrot, peeled

1 celery stalk

2 white onions

6 tbsp extra virgin olive oil, plus extra to serve

2 garlic cloves, lightly crushed

½ red chilli, finely chopped

1.2 litres (68 fl oz/ 5 cups) Vegetable or Chicken stock (bouillon) (see pages 115–116)

400 g (14 oz) tin cannellini beans, drained, or 100 g (3½ oz/½ cup) dried beans, cooked (see Borlotti Beans and Pasta Soup on page 122)

Handful of kale, chard or spinach

Salt and freshly ground black pepper

METHOD

Chop the pumpkin, carrot, celery and onion into 2 cm (¾ in) cubes. Heat the oil in a large saucepan over a medium heat and add the garlic and the cubed vegetables. Reduce the heat, cover with the lid and sweat for 20 minutes, shaking the pan frequently. Add the chilli (you can add more or less according to your taste) and fry for 2 minutes. Pour in the stock, increase the heat and bring to the boil. Reduce the heat and simmer for 30 minutes until the vegetables are tender. Stir in the beans and kale. Cook for 2–3 minutes until the kale is soft. Season to taste and serve with a swirl of your best olive oil.

PASTA E FASOI

Borlotti Beans and Pasta Soup

SERVES 8–10

This is the Venetian way of making this warming Italian classic. The herby oil is swirled into the soup before serving, or try pouring it over hot focaccia or steak. This version came from the chef Davide at Vini da Gigio where he uses beans from Lamon in the Dolomites, to the north-west of Venice.

METHOD

Put the beans into a large bowl, cover with cold water and leave to soak overnight at room temperature. Drain and set aside. Heat the 100 ml (31/2 fl oz/scant 1/2 cup) of oil over a medium heat in a large heavy-based saucepan and fry the Soffritto with the bay leaf and seasoning gently for 10–15 minutes until the vegetables start to soften and become translucent.

Add the stock and the beans to the pan and bring to the boil, stir through. Reduce the heat to a simmer so that the soup bubbles gently. Add the Parmesan rind and ham bone, if using. Skim off any foam and discard. Allow the soup to cook, stirring every now and again, for around 2 hours or until the beans are soft, adding more stock or hot water if necessary.

Remove from the heat and purée around three-quarters of the soup,

using a hand-held blender in the saucepan. It can all be puréed but I prefer to feel the texture of a few whole beans in contrast to the silky smooth soup.

Add the pasta to the soup, put the pan back over a medium heat and cook until the pasta is al dente. Taste and season as necessary. You may need to add a little more stock or hot water to maintain a soup consistency as the pasta will absorb the liquid.

Meanwhile, make the herb oil. Heat the 5 tablespoons of oil in a small saucepan and add the thyme, sage and rosemary. After 3–4 minutes when the herbs are infused (don't let them burn), pour most the oil through a small sieve into the soup and stir.

When the pasta is al dente, pour into warm bowls and serve with a swirl of the remaining herb oil and pepper.

500 g (1 lb 2 oz/ 2½ cups) dried borlotti (cranberry) beans (Lamon if you can find them)

100 ml (3½ fl oz/ scant ½ cup) extra virgin olive oil, plus 5 tbsp for the herb oil

1 quantity of Soffritto (see page 118)

1 bay leaf

Salt and freshly ground black pepper

1.5 litres (51 fl oz/ 6 cups) Vegetable or Chicken Stock (bouillon) (see pages 115–116), plus extra if needed

1 Parmesan rind (optional)

End of 1 leg of prosciutto or 1 ham bone (optional)

400 g (14 oz) small pasta shapes or broken spaghetti

Small handful of thyme sprigs

5 sage leaves

2 sprigs of rosemary

ZUPPA DI ORZO, CASTAGNE E PANCETTA

Bacon, Chestnut and Barley Soup

SERVES 6–8

Barley and chestnuts were staple winter foods at one time as they could be kept for months, often saving people from famine across Europe. Both, in my opinion, need a bit of a kick with flavour. In the Veneto you would be able to add the end of a leg of prosciutto but we have replaced that with bacon. With the addition of a Parmesan rind this becomes a flavourful, creamy, risotto-like soup that will bring comfort on the chilliest of days.

15 g (½ oz/1 tbsp) butter

3 tbsp good quality extra virgin olive oil, plus extra to serve

5 rashers (slices) streaky unsmoked bacon, finely chopped

1 quantity of Soffritto (see page 118)

2 garlic cloves, lightly crushed

1 bay leaf

1 long sprig of rosemary

Salt and freshly ground black pepper

1.5 litres (51 fl oz/6 cups) Chicken or Vegetable stock (bouillon) (see pages 115–116)

1 Parmesan rind

100 g (3½ oz/ ⅔ cup) cooked chestnuts

150 g (5½ oz/ ⅔ cup) pearl barley

30 g (1 oz) Parmesan, finely grated

METHOD

Heat the butter and oil over a medium heat in a large heavy-based saucepan and fry the bacon, Soffritto, garlic, bay leaf, rosemary and seasoning for 10–15 minutes until the vegetables start to soften and become translucent.

Add the stock and Parmesan rind to the pan, increase the heat and bring to the boil, stirring through. Crumble in half of the chestnuts and add the pearl barley. When the soup is spluttering, reduce the heat to a simmer so that is bubbles gently. Stir every now and again for around 25 minutes or until the barley is soft, adding more stock or hot water if necessary. Serve in warm bowls scattered with the remaining crumbled chestnuts, a swirl of oil, a little black pepper and the Parmesan.

Ada's Fish Soup with Saffron

SERVES 6

Ada Catto was head chef at the restaurant known locally as Alla Vedova, 'The Widow's Place', for 30 years. Married to a Venetian gondolier there is nothing she doesn't know about Venetian food. Ada's advice for fish soup is to choose what is fresh in the market and fished sustainably. She uses a mixture of monkfish, gurnard, shrimp, baby octopus, prawns, clams and mussels. Discard any broken shells and shellfish that remain open before cooking.

METHOD

In a large saucepan with a lid, heat the oil over a low heat and fry the onion, carrot, celery, garlic and chilli (add more or less to suit your taste) for around 15 minutes until softened. Add the tomato purée, a good pinch of pepper, the shellfish and wine and fry for 2–3 minutes, lid on, until the clams have opened.

Discard any clams that remain closed. Pour in the stock and saffron, increase the heat and bring to the boil. Add the fish and cook for 4–5 minutes, gently shaking the pan every now and again, until the fish is cooked through. Season with salt if necessary. Serve in bowls with bread.

6 tbsp extra virgin olive oil

1 small onion, finely chopped

1 small carrot, finely chopped

1 celery stalk, finely chopped

2 garlic cloves, left whole and lightly crushed

½ red chilli, finely chopped

2 tbsp tomato purée (tomato paste)

Freshly ground black pepper

12 medium prawns (shrimp), shells on

24 clams or mussels

50 ml (2 fl oz/½ cup) white wine

1 litre (34 fl oz/ 4¼ cups) fish or Seafood Stock (bouillon) (see page 117)

½ tsp saffron strands

1 kg (2 lb 4 oz) firm white fish, cleaned and chopped into bite-size pieces

Salt, to taste

Crusty white bread or sourdough, thickly sliced and toasted, to serve

RISO

Rice

In the Veneto, risotto tends to be wetter than in other parts of Italy and the rice remains just al dente; think of it as individual grains of rice in a creamy, wave of risotto. This is achieved partly with the use of vialone nano or carnaroli rice grains, which are less absorbent than arborio, the most commonly used risotto rice outside of Italy. Risotto is eaten as a first course in small portions and usually on its own so that you can appreciate its delicate, gentle flavour and texture.

As risotto waits for no man it is either made to order or certain Venetian restaurants and bars, such as Do Spade in San Polo, will make it at a specific time, so the locals know exactly when to turn up to relish it at its peak of perfection.

RISOTTO BASE A LA VELENZIANA

Basic Venetian Risotto

SERVES 4

After having watched the brilliant Mirko (left), the risotto chef at Da Romano restaurant on the island of Burano, here are our rules to make the perfect Venetian risotto.

A risotto is only as good as the stock (bouillon) you make it with. Use a homemade stock from trimmings that you would normally discard (see page 113). Have your heated stock ready by your risotto pan with a ladle to hand. If you have just made the stock and don't want to strain it yet (as you want to keep the rest cooking after using some), push a sieve into the pot to strain it and scoop ladlefuls from inside the sieve.

Have everything you need ready and within reach, so that you don't have to leave your risotto unattended while you find the cheese from the back of the refrigerator or find you have run out of wine.

2 tbsp extra virgin olive oil

50 g (2 oz/½ stick) butter

200 g (7 oz) leeks or spring onions (scallions) or shallots, finely sliced

1 celery stalk, finely chopped

Fine salt and freshly ground black, Sichuan or long pepper

300 g (10½ oz/ 1⅓ cup) vialone nano or other risotto rice

100 ml (3½ fl oz/ scant ½ cup) white wine

1.2 litres (40 fl oz/ 5 cups) stock (bouillon), warm (see pages 115–116)

50 g (1¾ oz) Parmesan, finely grated

METHOD

In a large saucepan, heat the oil and half the butter; the oil helps to stop the butter burning. When the butter has melted, soften the leeks and celery with salt and pepper over a low heat for around 10 minutes.

If you are making a risotto with other ingredients that need to be cooked, such as peas or mushrooms, add these at the same time as the leeks or onions, but if you are adding ingredients that don't want to be overcooked, such as fish, put these in towards the end.

Add the rice to the pan and allow it to 'toast' for around 3–5 minutes, stirring constantly, until all the grains are covered in the butter and oil.

Pour in the wine and allow to reduce for 2–3 minutes or until the strong smell of alcohol dissipates.

Ladle in around 500 ml (17 fl oz/ generous 2 cups) of the hot stock and mix quickly into the rice. Stir constantly with a wooden spoon and when the risotto thickens to the point where you can see the bottom of the pan when you draw the spoon across the bottom, add another ladleful of stock. Continue adding stock each time the risotto thickens back up.

After about 20 minutes, taste the risotto to see whether it is done. The rice grains should be just translucent through the grain. They should feel soft on the outside with a hint of firmness in the centre. Adjust the seasoning to taste. Remove the pan from the heat. Mirko cooks it *all'onda*, 'like a wave', leaving it slightly soupy as this liquid will continue to be absorbed over the following few minutes.

Beat in the remaining butter and the Parmesan, this will make your risotto creamy. Mirko tosses his risotto out of the pan into the air above, like waves splashing against the side of the boat (see opposite).

Cover the pan and allow the risotto to rest for around 3–5 minutes. Serve in warmed shallow bowls.

Lemon and Prosecco Risotto

Monica & Arianna GUEST RECIPE

SERVES 4

'If you can eat it, you can make a risotto out of it!' This is my friend Monica's mantra. She and her friend Arianna showed me this recipe. In Arianna's home risotto is eaten twice a week. It is a simple and filling answer to how to feed a family. She uses whatever vegetable she has in the house but her favourites are this lemon one or carrot risotto.

METHOD

Heat the oil and half the butter with a ladleful of stock in large saucepan and gently fry the leeks and shallot with some salt over a medium heat. Let them cook for 10–15 minutes or until soft. Add the rice to the pan and stir through, making sure it is coated in the buttery oil. Pour in the lemon juice and Prosecco, letting it evaporate for 2–3 minutes. Continue adding the stock and cooking the rice following the method in the basic recipe (see page 129), then add the lemon zest, rosemary and pepper. Turn off the heat, add the remaining butter and the Parmesan, and beat through with a wooden spoon to obtain a creamy consistency. Taste and season with salt, pepper or a little more lemon zest as necessary. Let the risotto sit with a lid over it for 2 minutes before serving.

VARIATIONS

PUMPKIN RISOTTO

Arianna says, 'Chop 350 g (12 oz) peeled, seeded pumpkin or butternut squash into 1 cm (½ in) dice and cook it in the pan with onions and a little of the stock until just soft.'

PEPPER RISOTTO

Add roughly chopped, roasted and peeled pepper (see page 156) to the pan with the onions.

BLACK RISOTTO

Use fish stock (bouillon) (see page 117) to make the risotto and add 2 tablespoons of cuttlefish ink to it when you add the first ladleful of stock. Cuttlefish ink (also called squid ink) is available online or at good Italian delis.

2 tbsp extra virgin olive oil

50 g (1¾ oz/ ½ stick) butter

1.2 litres (40 fl oz/ 5 cups) Chicken, Vegetable or light meat stock (bouillon), warm (see pages 115–116)

200 g (7 oz) leeks or spring onions (scallions), finely chopped

1 shallot, finely chopped

Fine salt

300 g (10½ oz/ 1⅓ cups) vialone nano or other risotto rice

Finely grated zest of 1 large unwaxed lemon and juice of 1½ lemons

100 ml (3½ fl oz/ scant ½ cup) Prosecco or white wine

1 sprig of rosemary, finely chopped

Freshly ground black, Sichuan or long pepper

50 g (1¾ oz) Parmesan, finely grated

RISOTTO AL PESCE AFFUMICATO

Smoked Fish Risotto

SERVES 4

Smoked herrings, what we call kippers, have been available in Venice since the Venetians started trading with northern countries. Preserved fish such as these travelled well and were popular in the past as part of the cuisine of the poor and were eaten with polenta. I loved the idea of making a creamy risotto with smoked fish and after listening to our friend Monica's words about making a risotto out of 'anything you can eat' it has now become one of my favourite dishes, being both easy to make and full of flavour. A simple stock (bouillon) is made from the cooking liquor for the kipper.

METHOD

Heat the milk and water in a saucepan over a medium heat and when simmering hot (don't let it boil), add the kippers and cook through. Strain the liquid into another saucepan and keep warm; this will be your stock. Remove and discard the skin and flake up the fish into a bowl. Follow the instructions for the basic risotto (see page 129), mixing in the fish at the end before the Parmesan and remaining butter is added. Serve with extra Parmesan and the parsley.

200 ml (7 fl oz/ scant 1 cup) milk

1 litre (34 fl oz/ 4¼ cups) water

4 kippers (around 400 g/14 oz)

2 tbsp extra virgin olive oil

50 g (2 oz/½ stick) butter

200 g (7 oz) leeks or spring onions (scallions) or shallots, finely sliced

1 celery stalk, finely chopped

Fine salt and freshly ground black, Sichuan or long pepper

300 g (10½ oz/ 1⅓ cups) vialone nano or other risotto rice

100 ml (3½ fl oz/ scant ½ cup) white wine

50 g (1¾ oz) Parmesan, finely grated, plus extra to serve

Handful of parsley, roughly chopped

RISOTTO ALLA SBIRRAGLIA

Cop's Chicken Risotto

SERVES 6–8

This rich chicken risotto has become a family favourite; it's packed with flavour, inexpensive, and fills up hungry teenagers and fussy adults alike. I love to think that this recipe has been doing just that for a few hundred years, feeding Venetian families who named it *risotto alla sbirraglia* after the military police called the *sbirri*. No one really knows why, it could be that policemen were known to pinch a chicken or two on their nightly rounds. Some recipes for this dish contain beef, so I have suggested using beef stock, which enriches it further without the cost.

METHOD

Prepare the Soffritto following the instructions on page 118 and fry it in the olive oil over a low heat with the garlic, rosemary and pancetta in a large heavy-based pan for around 10 minutes or until the vegetables are soft. Season the chicken and, in another pan, fry it on all sides in the sunflower oil until the skin is crisp and golden brown. Transfer the chicken into the softened Soffritto. Discard the sunflower oil. Add the wine to the chicken and allow it to evaporate for 2 minutes, then pour in 1 litre (34 fl oz/4¼ cups) of the stock. Bring to the boil and cook, covered, for 10 minutes.

Pour in the rice and stir through. Continue to cook, stirring and moving the chicken and rice around the pan every now and again. As the stock is absorbed, add more as necessary to loosen it. It should be a flowing, creamy consistency. This will take around 25–30 minutes. As soon as the rice and chicken are both cooked, take the pan off the heat. Mix in the Parmesan and butter. Remove from the heat and let it stand, covered, for a few minutes. Serve in warm bowls.

1 quantity of Soffritto (see page 118)

8 tbsp extra virgin olive oil

2 garlic cloves, lightly crushed

1 sprig of rosemary

6 slices of pancetta or bacon, unsmoked, cut into small dice

1 whole medium chicken, jointed, or 8 large chicken thighs on the bone

4 tbsp sunflower oil

100 ml (3½ fl oz/ scant ½ cup) white wine

300 g (10 1½ oz/ 1⅓ cups) carnaroli or vialone nano rice

1–1.2 litres (34–40 fl oz/ 4¼–5 cups) beef, Chicken or Vegetable stock (bouillon) (see pages 115–116)

50 g (1¾ oz) Parmesan, finely grated

30 g (1 oz/2 tbsp) salted butter

Rice and Peas

SERVES 8

More of a soup than a risotto, *risi e bisi* is traditionally a springtime dish when the new peas are at their best. The earliest record of it is in the 1500s when it became known as the dish for the Doge. It was made on 25 April on the feast of San Marco. Under the Austro-Hungarian occupation in the 1800s, strawberries were temporarily added to *risi e bisi* as a political protest. The three colours – green, white and red – were the colours of the tricolore, the flag of the united Italy.

Lele, from the famous restaurant Buso la Torre on the glass-making island of Murano, told us that he picks peas from his garden and uses the pods to make the stock (bouillon). He grows enough to freeze so he can make *risi e bisi* all year round. In the absence of home-grown peas, we found this recipe one of the hardest to perfect for the book. No matter what peas, frozen or fresh, we used or what we used to make the stock, such as mangetout (snow peas) and sugar snap peas, we just couldn't get a flavour we were happy with. Giancarlo suggested using tinned peas, which I didn't think fitted the romantic image of the recipe using spring's fresh new peas. However, he insisted on having a go and I have to admit, through clenched teeth, he was right. Bingo, it's delicious, everything it should be, full of flavour and terribly moreish.

3 tbsp extra virgin olive oil

50 g (1¾ oz/ ½ stick) salted butter

1 medium white onion, finely chopped

50 g (1¾ oz) pancetta or bacon, cut into 5 mm (¼ in) dice

450 g (1 lb) tinned peas, drained

300 g (10½ oz/ 1⅓ cups) vialone nano or other risotto rice

1.2–1.5 litres (40–51 fl oz/ 5–6 cups) Chicken or hamstock (bouillon) (see page 116)

100 g (3½ oz) Parmesan, finely grated

Fine salt

Handful of parsley, finely chopped

METHOD

Heat the oil and half the butter in a large heavy-based saucepan over a medium heat. Add the onion and bacon and fry gently for 5–10 minutes until the onion is soft, then add the peas. Follow the instructions for the basic risotto (see page 129), adding enough stock so that it is a really soupy consistency. Don't add the salt, however, until you have added all the Parmesan; taste first and add the salt if needed. Serve in warm bowls with parsley and eat with a spoon.

RISOTTO DI GAMBERI

Prawn Risotto

SERVES 4 AS A MAIN OR 6 AS A STARTER

At Trattoria La Madonna they are well known for their seafood risotto. I remember years ago they used to ring a huge ship's bell when it was served and everyone flooded into the restaurant to have the risotto. The locals would know to arrive ten minutes before, get seated, have a drink and wait for the sound of the bell. Teams of waiters rushed between the huge cooking pot and the tables. Nowadays the bell has gone but they still serve it at particular times to ensure it is at peak condition when it arrives at the table – you wait for the risotto, it doesn't wait for you. The seafood risotto, their signature dish, is really creamy and made buttery with a little Parmesan. Seafood is mixed with a light stock on a base of celery and onion, no carrots, as it would spoil the colour.

The base is made from gently frying onions and celery, including the leaves, which have so much flavour. Do try and find prawns (shrimp) that are raw, they will probably have been frozen and that's fine but you need the shells and heads for the stock or the flavour just won't be the same.

650 g (1 lb 7 oz) raw medium prawns (shrimp), shells on

3 tbsp olive oil

2 celery stalks with leaves, finely chopped

1 medium white onion, finely chopped

300 g (10½ oz/ 1⅓ cups) carnaroli or other risotto rice

50 ml (2 fl oz/ ¼ cup) white wine

1.2 litres (40 fl oz/ 5 cups) Seafood Stock (bouillon) (see page 117)

30 g (1 oz) Parmesan, finely grated

METHOD

Peel the prawns and make a stock from their heads and shells (see page 117). If the prawns are large, cut them into bite-size pieces. Place in a bowl and reserve in the refrigerator for later. Follow the instructions for the basic risotto on page 129, adding the prawns halfway through cooking the rice. Serve in warm bowls.

FAGIOLI

Beans

Beans in their dried state are a relatively new ingredient in my cupboard. While testing bean soup recipes with our chef Antonio Sanzone, he convinced me that a bean soup should only ever be made with dried beans. The flavour and velvety texture of a bean that has been dried, soaked and cooked is infinitely better than one lurking in the murky waters of a tin. I instantly became an enthusiastic convert to the pulse and now go about preaching to others of their virtues. An inexpensive and valuable source of protein that we just don't use enough of in the UK, all they need is a little forethought.

For some years I was confused by the terms pulse, legume and bean. Pulse is from the Latin word *puls* meaning a porridge-like substance made from beans or grains. The Roman word *legumen* meant any edible seeds that form in pods. From this the French then took legume to mean any vegetable and so we took pulse to mean the dried seed or bean that had to be soaked before cooking such as broad (fava) beans, borlotti (cranberry), lentils, peas and chickpeas (garbanzos).

The choice of beans in the Veneto is wide, with many people growing their own in the country. They are used fresh and immature in summer for salads and *contorni* – vegetable side dishes – and mature and dried throughout winter for soups.

Many of the chefs we spoke to in Venice were very particular about the beans they used, how they were grown and where they came from. The town of Lamon, in the valley of Belluno, north of Venice, is the main area for growing beans and has been since the mid-1500s. The Slow Food organisation has protected some of the varieties from extinction, such as the spagnolit and the yellow gialet. These are hard to get outside the Veneto but delis and health food shops are a good place to look for unusual varieties.

For some reason packets of beans often miss off the cooking instructions but most beans react in the same way. Dried beans will deliver much better flavour than tinned ones, so if time permits it's always preferable to use soaked dried beans. Here are our tips on making the most of your dried beans:

- Choose recently harvested and dried beans if you see a date on the packet. Their skins become tougher the older they are.

- Pick over the beans discarding any stones or broken beans. Wash them in cold water.

- To speed up the cooking time and help the beans hold their shape, soak in plenty of cold water so that they are well covered; small beans for around 4 hours to overnight and large, like butter (lima) beans, for at least 8 hours.

- To speed up the soaking process put the washed beans in a saucepan of plenty of cold water and bring to the boil. Boil for 2 minutes and remove from the heat. Cover and let them soak for 1 hour, or until swollen and the skins are softened.

- Beans can be cooked slowly in the oven. Preheat the oven to 160°C (320°F/Gas 3). Rinse the soaked beans and discard any broken ones. Put the beans and any flavourings, such as onion and garlic, into a heavy-based, flameproof casserole and pour in enough cold water to cover them by 3 cm (1¼ in). Bring to the boil and boil rapidly for 10 minutes to remove toxins. Cover with the lid and cook in the oven for 45 minutes to 1 hour. Add 1 teaspoon of salt. Put the lid back on and continue to cook for a further 45 minutes to 1 hour or until cooked through.

- If you cook the beans on the hob, make sure they are covered with 5 cm (2 in) fresh cold salted water in a heavy-based pan. Flavour the beans with one or two of the following: 1 bay leaf, 2 sage leaves, 1 sprig of thyme, 1 onion or 1 garlic clove. Bring to the boil and boil rapidly for 10 minutes, then gently simmer until tender, stirring occasionally. Make sure they are always submerged in water, so add more as necessary.

- Soften tough skins with a teaspoon of bicarbonate of soda (baking soda) 10 minutes before the end of cooking time.

- The cooking time will vary hugely, so check the beans regularly. To give you an idea, after soaking, small beans take around 1 hour and large beans take around 1½ hours.

- When the beans are cooked, leave them to cool in their cooking liquid. They will keep in the refrigerator for up to 5 days.

- For soups, or when serving with fish or meat, purée one-third of the beans with a hand-held blender for a slightly thicker consistency. They can also be puréed completely to a velvety cream.

- If serving them as they are for a vegetable dish, dress the beans with your best peppery extra virgin olive oil, pepper and salt. A little wine vinegar or lemon juice gives a little acidity and they always look pretty with chopped parsley.

INSALATA DI FAVE, ASPARAGI E ZUCCHINI

Broad Bean, Asparagus and Courgette Salad

SERVES 4 AS A MAIN OR 6 AS A STARTER

Apparently Pythagoras hated broad (fava) beans so much that rather than escape through a bean field, he opted to be captured and killed by his enemies in 500 BC in the village Metapontum in Basilicata aged around 75 years old. If he had eaten this salad it may all have been different. The idea for this recipe comes from Francesco at the La Cantina; he loves to add different flavours to a dish around the edge of the plate. White asparagus originated from Bassano, south of Venice. A terrible storm is said to have damaged the asparagus crop, so a local farmer dug up the white and tender new shoots that hadn't yet emerged from the ground. He sold these and they have been popular ever since. In Bassano, asparagus is eaten with hard-boiled eggs. I like to put the ingredients separately on the plate so you can try the different combinations.

2 courgettes (zucchini), finely sliced into ribbons

6 tbsp extra virgin olive oil

3 hen's eggs or 6 quail's eggs

200 g (7 oz/ generous 1 cup) fresh or frozen broad (fava) beans

2 tbsp mint leaves, shredded

1 tbsp lemon juice

Salt and freshly ground black, cubeb or pink pepper

300 g (10½ oz) white or green asparagus

30 g (1 oz) Parmesan shavings

30 g (1 oz/¼ cup) flaked (slivered) almonds, toasted

6 dessert spoons Parmesan and Ricotta Pesto (see page 33)

METHOD

Preheat the oven to 180°C (350°F/ Gas 4). Lay the courgette ribbons onto baking parchment on a baking tray and brush with 2 tablespoons of the oil. Season and roast for 5 minutes, remove from the tray and set aside.

Cook the eggs in boiling water until just hard-boiled, around 8–10 minutes for the hen's eggs and 4–6 minutes for quail's eggs. Drain the eggs and run under cold water. Tap them to break the shells; this will stop the blue ring appearing around the yolks. Leave in very cold water to cool. Boil the broad beans in salted water until tender, between 3–6 minutes depending on how mature they are. Remove from the heat, drain the beans and plunge them into a bowl of cold water. Pop them out of their wrinkly shells and add them to the courgettes with the mint leaves, lemon juice and 2 tablespoons of the oil. Toss gently. Season to taste.

Bend the asparagus stems so that the woody ends snap off; discard. Steam or boil the tips for 3–6 minutes until tender, then plunge into a bowl of cold water to stop them cooking. Drain and set aside. To assemble, put the courgette and broad bean salad on one side, the asparagus dressed with the Parmesan shavings and almonds on another, and a pile of the eggs separately. Season the asparagus and eggs with salt and drizzle over a little oil. Add a spoonful of the Parmesan and Ricotta Pesto onto each plate, drizzle with the remaining oil and a sprinkling of pepper.

INSALATA DI FAGIOLI SPAGNOLI E MENTUCCIA

Butter Bean and Mint Salad

SERVES 4-6

Butter (lima) beans are a newcomer to my diet but now I am hooked. They are really good for you, filling and inexpensive – what more could you want! Their velvety smoothness makes a creamy contrast to grilled meats and crunchy vegetables. This recipe is good with cannellini or haricot (navy) beans too but you will have to adjust the cooking time. I cook them from dried while I have meat cooking long and slow in the oven. It gives the same result as soaking the beans first, but it does mean they have a longer cooking time.

METHOD

Preheat the oven to 160°C (320°F/ Gas 3). Rinse the beans in cold water and discard any broken ones. Put them into a heavy-based flameproof casserole dish and pour in enough cold water to cover them by 3 cm (1¼ in). Add 1 teaspoon of salt, the onion and garlic clove and stir through. Bring to the boil and boil rapidly for 10 minutes. Cover with the lid and cook in the oven for 1 hour. Stir the beans through and check if they are tender. Depending on how old they are and how they were dried, their cooking time can vary; they may need up to 1 more hour, but check again every 15 minutes. As soon as they are tender all the way through, drain and pour the beans into a serving dish.

Soak the onions in cold water to dilute their strength for 10 minutes, drain, dry on paper towels and tip into the beans. Pour over the oil, a little extra salt as required, a good twist of black pepper (I loosen my pepper mill to get some good crunchy pieces of pepper) and the mint and toss through while the beans are still warm. Serve straight away or allow to cool to room temperature. Scatter with parsley just before serving.

VARIATION

Add a few baby spinach leaves and crumbled feta to the bean salad to make it more of a main meal.

200 g (7 oz/1 cup) dried butter (lima) beans

Fine salt and freshly ground black pepper

1 small onion, peeled and halved

1 fat garlic clove, skin on

4 spring onions (scallions) or 1 small red onion, finely chopped

3 tbsp extra virgin olive oil

Handful of mint leaves, shredded

Handful of parsley leaves, roughly chopped (optional)

At the Rialto Market

In all the years that Giancarlo and I have been travelling around Italy, a noisy, busy market still thrills us. Giancarlo joins in with the banter and I quietly shop or photograph the produce admiring the variety, colours and unfamiliar cultivars. Shopping at the market keeps you in touch with the seasons as the ingredients are still local – look out for labels saying *nostrano*, meaning 'our local produce'. There can be no harder crowd to please than the mammas of Italy so you can be sure of the quality.

The market garden of Venice is the island of Sant'Erasmo, the largest island in the lagoon with acres set aside for an endless supply of vegetables, including artichokes, peas and broad (fava) beans, destined for the homes and restaurants of the city. As well as fresh produce, look out for sun-dried peppers and tomatoes (see page 38 for ideas on what to do with them), precious porcini mushrooms and twisting fingers of purple radicchio.

VERDURE ALLA GRIGLIA

Grilled Vegetables

Platters of grilled aubergines (eggplants) and courgettes (zucchini) glistening with precious green olive oil are on every bar in Venice. My favourites were in the restaurant Alla Vedova, they weren't at all oily but light to eat, quickly grilled and scattered with basil leaves.

METHOD

Preheat the oven to 200°C (400°F/Gas 6). Slice vegetables into discs or lengths about 1 cm (½ in) thick and lay them on a baking tray lined with baking parchment. Try to get equal-size slices so they cook evenly. Season with salt and pepper. Give them a light brushstroke of good extra virgin olive oil and cook for around 20–25 minutes. Serve at room temperature with torn basil leaves and just a few drops of your best extra virgin olive oil.

FRITTATA
Frittata

I am slightly mad for frittatas. It took a while after being put off by a horrible incident when I set fire to a pan of undercooked frittata and managed to put the whole hob out of use during a contest on stage at a food show in South Africa. My team, which included the Hairy Bikers and Brian Turner, was not impressed. However, I am over it now, some years on, just. Anyway the humble frittata has become popular in our home since we both started eating less bread. Now when I cook broccoli, roast vegetables or courgettes (zucchini), I always make more than we need knowing the following day they will be my breakfast. I also make a frittata if I have guests, cutting it into wedges while still warm and offering it around on a plate. It keeps them going if I am running late with dinner, which I usually am.

As the anonymous 14th century chef the Anonimo Veneziano wrote below, they are simple:

'Herbatella etc. If you want to make a herb dish cooked in a frying pan. Take mint, sage, parsley, marjoram and every good herb that you may have. Grind everything together in a mortar with lard and temper with eggs, and cook it thus in a frying pan with fat.'

FRITTATA SEMPLICE

Basic Frittata

SERVES 2 FOR LUNCH OR 8 AS *CICCHETTI*

This is our standard recipe. For other flavours, add large handfuls of chopped herbs, marinated artichokes, cooked asparagus, cooked broccoli or roasted peppers to the cooked onion. Be generous with the flavourings and seasoning. Use a small non-stick frying pan and don't stint on the oil or it won't turn out easily.

METHOD

In a small non-stick frying pan, heat the oil and fry the onion gently until soft. Beat the eggs in a bowl with the Parmesan and season. Pour into the pan and cook for 2 minutes over a low heat. Use a heatproof spatula to make holes in the frittata to allow the runny egg to get to the pan. Continue to cook and when most of the egg is set, put a large plate over the pan, and bravely and decisively flip it over so the frittata comes out of the pan and onto the plate. Now slide the frittata back into the pan to cook the other side for 2 minutes. It should be slightly soft inside and lightly browned outside. Slide the frittata onto a warm plate. Serve drizzled with a good olive oil, a fresh grating of Parmesan and a scatter of black pepper.

3 tbsp extra virgin olive oil, plus extra to serve

1 medium onion, or 1 handful of spring onions (scallions), finely chopped

4 eggs

30 g (1 oz) Parmesan, finely grated

Salt and freshly ground black pepper

PEPERONI AL FORNO

Roasted
Red Peppers

Blacken whole red peppers in the oven.
Heat the oven to 180°C (350°F/Gas 4)
and roast on a baking tray for about
45 minutes. I do them regularly while
I'm cooking something else. If you are
in a hurry, you can speed up the process
by cooking at 220°C (425°F/Gas 7) for
25–30 minutes. Remove from the oven
and allow the peppers to sweat in a clean
plastic bag or in a bowl covered in cling
film (plastic wrap). When cool, peel
off the skins, dress and store them as
the sun-dried tomatoes, or use them
straight away.

They are great cut into strips and rolled
around bocconcini, the tiny balls of
mozzarella, and a basil leaf (see page 38).

SALSA DI PEPERONI ROSSI ARROSTITI

Roasted Red Pepper Sauce

SERVES 4

This is such an easy and healthy sauce. I nearly always have a jar of it in the refrigerator. It's wonderful with creamy mozzarella, goat's cheese, or heated and served with fish.

METHOD

To make a red pepper sauce, blend 100 g (3½ oz) rehydrated sun-dried peppers or roasted fresh, peeled peppers with 100 ml (3½ fl oz/ scant ½ cup) extra virgin olive oil, 1 teaspoon white wine vinegar, a small peeled garlic clove, freshly ground black pepper and a pinch of salt, if needed. Taste and, if necessary, add 1 teaspoon sugar. Serve this drizzled over burrata, a creamy mozzarella-style cheese, or buffalo mozzarella or white fish such as pan-fried sea bass.

At the Rialto Market

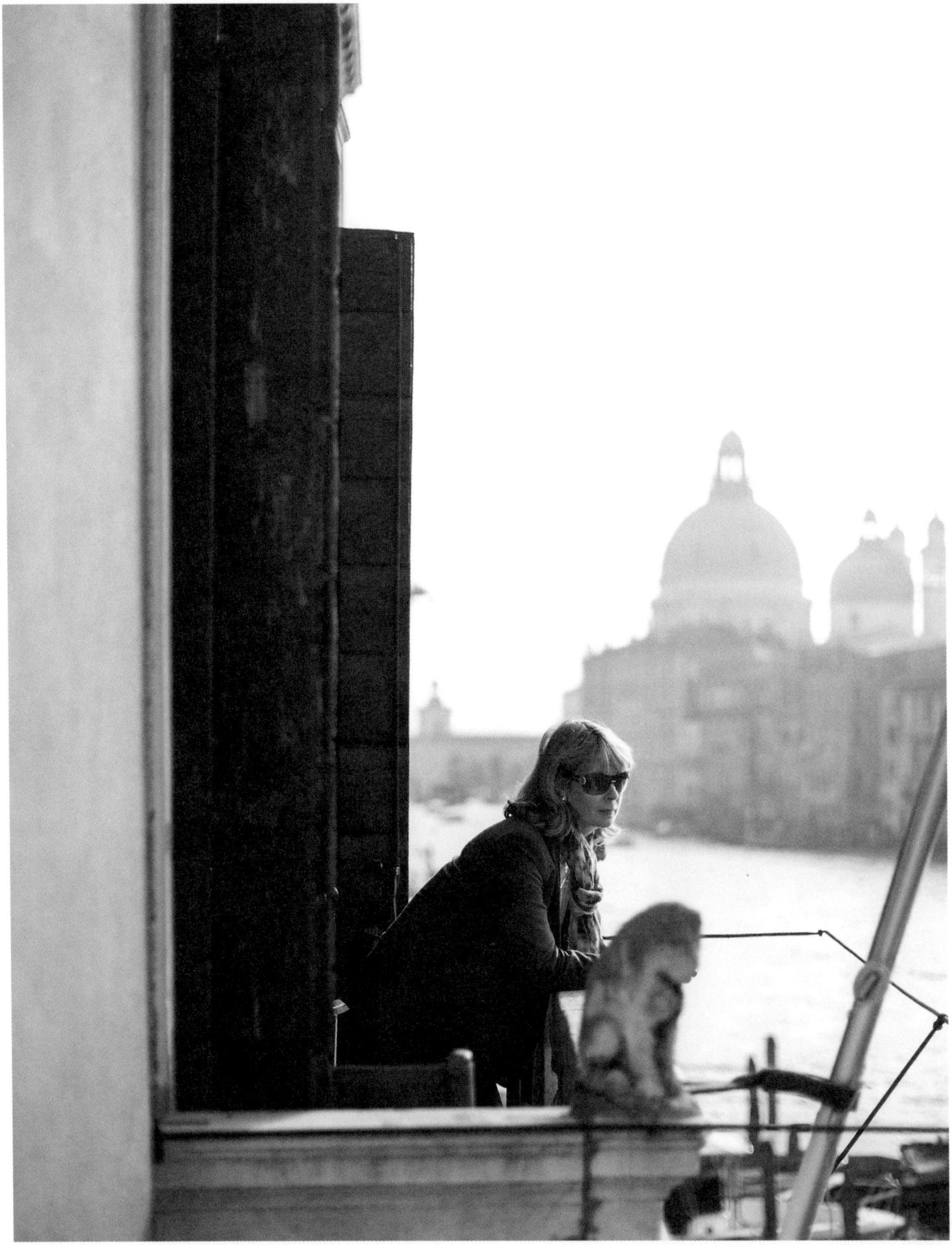

PEPERONATA

Red Peppers, Aubergines and Onions

SERVES 6–8

Made all over Italy, and as colourful as the *carnevale* itself, the difference with a Venetian peperonata is that it contains aubergines (eggplants), and for a touch of medieval spice we have added a stick of cinnamon. We love it with white fish, steak or with a poached egg on top. Try it too as a chutney with cheese. 'Everyone has their own recipe,' I was told by a couple of Venetian women. I took them at their word and we invented our own version with roasted aubergines.

4 red (bell) peppers

1 knob of butter

6 tbsp extra virgin olive oil

3 small white onions, cut into half moons

1 cinnamon stick, around 2.5 cm (1 in) long

1 garlic clove, whole, lightly crushed

Salt and freshly ground black pepper

1 aubergine (eggplant), sliced into 1 cm (½ in) circles

Small handful of parsley or basil leaves, roughly chopped

METHOD

Preheat the oven to 180°C (350°F/Gas 4). Roast the peppers whole following the instructions on page 156.

Meanwhile, heat the butter and 4 tablespoons of the oil in a frying pan over a low heat and sweat the onions with the cinnamon, garlic and seasoning for around 10 minutes or until soft and translucent. Make sure the onions don't burn or take on any colour. Remove from the heat and set aside.

Lay the aubergine slices on a baking tray, brush with the rest of the oil and roast in the oven for 20–30 minutes until they are golden and are soft to the touch.

Peel the skin from the peppers and discard the stalk, seeds and pith. Tear the peppers into strips and lay onto a serving dish. Add a layer of the onions, followed by a layer of aubergines. Repeat the layers, seasoning lightly in between each layer and pour over any oil from the pan of onions. Let the dish sit for 1 hour or so, or overnight if you have time, to let the juices amalgamate and improve the flavour. Just before serving, garnish with the parsley or basil and another good twist of black pepper. Serve at room temperature.

CARCIOFI

Artichokes

Tiny purple artichokes called castraure come from Sant'Erasmo, the market produce island off Venice, in early spring. At the market the traders prepare them as they wait for customers, putting the trimmed little artichoke bottoms into buckets of cold water. These are boiled and used in risotto, pies, frittata, *tramezzini* and *cicchetti*.

CARCIOFI MARINATI

Marinated Artichokes

MAKES AROUND 1 KG (2 LB 4 OZ)

If you are lucky enough to be able to grow or buy small tender artichokes, by all means get chopping and marinate some. Be brutal. Hard leaves never soften and spoil the experience of eating wonderfully soft, delicately flavoured artichokes.

METHOD

Pull away all the tough leaves from the artichokes and trim the stems to around 5 cm (2 in), then use sharp scissors to cut away the tips of the remaining leaves, losing almost half their length. Remove the fluffy chokes, if they have them, with a small teaspoon. As you prepare each artichoke, put it into a large bowl of cold water with the juice of 1 lemon squeezed into it to prevent them becoming black while you prepare them all. Bring a large saucepan of salted water and vinegar to the boil with a ratio of one-third vinegar to two-thirds water. Cook the artichokes whole until tender. Depending on their size, this could take up to 45 minutes. Remove and drain, stalks pointing upwards, on a tea towel (dish cloth). Transfer into a clean container with the peppercorns and top with the remaining lemon juice and some olive oil, making sure they are covered. Store in the refrigerator for up to 2 weeks.

1.5 kg (3 lb 5 oz) artichokes

Juice of 2 lemons

Fine salt

White wine vinegar

10 black peppercorns

Extra virgin olive oil

ROMANESCO ALLE SPEZIE CON UVETTA

Spiced Cauliflower or Broccoli with Raisins

SERVES 6

I have been rooting around trying to find suitable Renaissance vegetable dishes that made good use of the spices around at the time. It seems although 14th century chef the Anonimo Veneziano and others made notes of the main courses, vegetables were often forgotten from contemporary cookbooks. This and the Buttered Carrot with Herbs on page 167 are loosely based on similar recipes in Apicius, a collection of early Roman cookery. They both work very well with spicy dishes such as Chicken with Ginger, Saffron and Dates (page 221), and the Fantastic Chicken with Fennel and Fine Spices (page 223), and also with roast meats. I use the pointy green cauliflower called romanesco when I can find it but white cauliflower, broccoli and all cabbages work well with the recipe too. As for the raisins, try to find the little packets sold as snacks that contain semi-dried green, red and brown raisins and sultanas, they have a wonderful flavour and are really pretty with the green vegetables.

3 tbsp raisins

100 ml (3½ fl oz/ scant ½ cup) sweet wine such as Madeira, Vin Santo or Muscat

1 shallot or ½ medium white onion, finely chopped

1 garlic clove, whole, peeled and lightly crushed

50 g (1¾ oz/ ½ stick) salted butter

3 tbsp olive oil

1 tbsp cumin seeds

2 tbsp coriander seeds

500 g (1 lb 2 oz) cauliflower or broccoli, cut into bite-size florets, or cabbage, roughly chopped

Salt and freshly ground black pepper

METHOD

Soak the raisins in the sweet wine for at least 30 minutes and up to overnight. Fry the onion and garlic in the butter and oil in a large frying pan over a low heat until soft. Dry fry the cumin and coriander seeds in a small pan for just 1–2 minutes or until they smell fragrant (don't let them burn) and then crush in a pestle and mortar to a fine powder. Add to the onion. Add the raisins and their liquor to the onion and keep warm over a very low heat.

Steam or boil the florets or leaves for 2–4 minutes until just tender, drain and add to the pan with the onion and toss to combine. Season to taste, discard the garlic and serve warm.

CAROTE SALTATE AL BURRO CON ERBE

Buttered Carrots with Herbs

SERVES 6–8

This colourful and easy carrot recipe goes with almost any fish, chicken or meat dish. The cinnamon gives the carrots a nutty background flavour before they are coated in a herby, garlicky butter.

METHOD

Steam or boil the carrots until just soft. Meanwhile, melt the butter in a large frying pan with a lid and fry the garlic and cinnamon for just 1–2 minutes over a low heat, making sure they don't burn. Drain the carrots, add to the garlic butter and stir to combine. Cover the pan and continue to cook for 5 minutes, shaking the pan frequently. Season to taste and scatter over the herbs. Toss to combine and serve warm.

500 g (1 lb 2 oz) carrots, peeled if muddy, cut into 5 × 1 cm (2 × ½ in) batons

50 g (1¾ oz/ ½ stick) salted butter

1 fat garlic clove, finely chopped

1 small cinnamon stick, around 5 cm (2 in) long

Salt and freshly ground black pepper

Handful of chives, finely chopped

Large handful of fresh coriander (cilantro), roughly chopped

CAVOLO NERO E MELE

Black Kale and Apple

SERVES 4–6

I learnt this combination from Dimitri Gris, the chef at Il Covino. He is from Belluno where the famous Lamon beans come from. There is a history of smoked meat in the area and so he serves this dish with smoked pork. It's also great with sausages or the turkey roll on page 218. If you can't get hold of cavolo nero, you can use green kale instead.

METHOD

Cook the apples with the water in a saucepan until just soft and take off the heat. Remove any thick stalks from the cavolo nero before roughly chopping into slices. In a separate large saucepan, boil or steam the kale for around 3–4 minutes until soft. Heat the butter in a large frying pan and add the apples and kale. Fry together for 3–4 minutes, season to taste and serve.

2 eating (dessert) apples, peeled, cored and thinly sliced

4 tbsp water

200 g (7 oz) cavolo nero

50 g (1¾ oz/ ½ stick) salted butter

Salt and freshly ground black pepper

SALSA DI CREN

Horseradish Sauce

SERVES 6

I always think of the very English combination of horseradish sauce and roast beef, but it is popular in Venice too. Horseradish grows wild and is cultivated in the far north of Italy, and is often eaten with strongly-flavoured fish and roast lamb. We have used it in the recipe for Black and White Polenta squares on page 34.

METHOD

Finely grate a stick of fresh horseradish into a bowl. Do this at arm's length as it's strong stuff and a sudden inhalation will make your nose burn. Mix in the vinegar, lemon juice, sugar, salt and cream to taste and serve in a little bowl. You can store the horseradish in the refrigerator for up to 3 days in a sealed jar.

50 g (1¾ oz) fresh horseradish

2–3 tsp white wine vinegar

1–2 tsp lemon juice

1–2 tsp caster (superfine) sugar

Fine salt

2–3 tbsp crème fraîche or double (heavy) cream

VERZA AFFOGATA

Smothered Green Cabbage

SERVES 4

There are many versions of this recipe in different Venetian cookbooks, most telling you to leave the cabbage suffocated in beef or chicken stock (bouillon) for an hour or two on the stove. I have tried this and although the cabbage tastes interesting, it is reduced to an otherworldly pale brown substance that you wouldn't serve to your enemy. Maybe this method was developed to preserve the cabbage. However, cabbage is now readily available, so I would rather cook it quickly, preserving the colour and the vitamins as well as the texture. Do try and find lardo di colonnata, which is back fat from the pig that has been pressed and preserved with rosemary and salt. A block of it will last ages in your refrigerator and it really does give a wonderful flavour to stews, soups and vegetable dishes. It is usually sliced very thinly and it melts even with just the heat of a candle. In this case, a pesto, or paste, is made from the chopped lardo, garlic and rosemary and this melted paste is used to fry the cabbage. If you can't find lardo, use good unsmoked streaky bacon.

500 g (1 lb 2 oz) green cabbage, any variety

100 g (3½ oz) Lardo di colonnata or unsmoked, fatty streaky bacon

2 garlic cloves

1 sprig of rosemary

3 tbsp olive oil

3 tbsp white wine

Salt and freshly ground pepper to taste

METHOD

Cut the stalk away from the cabbage and finely shred it into thin slices. Using a large knife, chop the lardo, garlic and rosemary leaves – discard the stalk – together on a board until they are well blended and the mixture forms a paste. Heat the oil and paste together in a large wok or frying pan with a lid. Stir-fry the mixture for 2 minutes, then throw in the cabbage and toss it through the fat. Add the wine, cover the pan and continue to cook for up to 20 minutes or until the cabbage is how you like it; still green and bouncy or soft and wilted. Season to taste. Serve straight away or keep warm until you are ready.

RADICI AL FORNO

Roasted Root Vegetables

SERVES 4–6

Giancarlo loves the colours and flavours of this dish. It's a far cry from the roasted vegetables of his beloved Tuscany where (bell) peppers, courgettes (zucchini) and aubergines (eggplants) ruled the day. Autumn and winter in Venice, as in the UK, it is all about the roots.

METHOD

Preheat the oven to 180°C (350°F/ Gas 4). Scrub and clean the root vegetables, leaving the skins on unless very muddy, in which case peel them. Cut into batons or wedges around 1.5 cm (⅔ in) thick, so that the vegetables are all around the same size and they have the same cooking time. Toss with the oil, garlic and seasoning in a mixing bowl. Do season generously. Roast in a baking tray for around 30 minutes or until cooked through.

700 g (1 lb 9 oz) root vegetables, such as beetroot (red beets), parsnips, celeriac (celery root) and carrots

4 tbsp extra virgin olive oil

8 garlic cloves, skin on, lightly crushed

Salt and freshly ground black pepper

ZUCCA
Pumpkin

Pumpkin – or winter squashes – found popularity relatively recently in Venice as it was deemed food for the poor, although it grows easily in the Po Valley. Here in the UK, we mainly have the incredibly popular cream-coloured butternut squash and the tasteless bright orange Halloween pumpkin, only occasionally seeing other varieties. In the Veneto, the flavourful pumpkins to use are the monstrous, knobbly variety known as zucca barucca, which by the sound of it really should be used as a missile, and the smooth green mantovana, which is also popular for its bright orange flesh. Pumpkins are used for pasta fillings (see page 102), gnocchi (see page 104), soup (see page 118) and risotto (see page 133), fried and dipped in sugar, candied, sold on the streets, for roasted seeds, sweet pumpkin pies, as vegetables to go with fish and meat, and more.

ZUCCA IN SAOR

Pumpkin in Saor

At the restaurant L'Osteria Santa Marina, the kataifi pastry-wrapped prawns are served on a circle of pumpkin in saor. You can make these by layering steamed or fried pumpkin with Sweet and Sour Onions (see page 41), using the ratio of 3 parts onion to 1 part pumpkin.

PURÈ DI ZUCCA ARROSTITA

Roast Pumpkin Purée

SERVES 6–8 (MAKES 600 G/1 LB 5 OZ)

Our chefs, Antonio Sanzone and Daniele Malagni, came up with this idea when thinking of seasonal vegetables to serve with the popular sea bass on our menu. The flesh becomes sweeter still after roasting and the colour is beautiful contrasted with the white fish and a helping of Black Kale and Apple (see page 168). It is also gorgeous with roast meat, Pot Roast Game in Wine (see page 206) and sausages.

METHOD

Preheat the oven to 180°C (350°F/Gas 4). Peel and halve the pumpkin, scoop out the seeds and discard along with the peelings (or put both into a freezer bag and freeze to use later with other peelings to make stock (bouillon) on page 115). Cut the flesh into 3 cm (1¼ in) cubes and put them in a foil-lined baking tray. Break the bulb of garlic into cloves, leaving the skins on, and scatter them over the pumpkin. Pour over the oil, season and mix everything together to coat the pumpkin. Cover the tray with foil and roast for 40 minutes. Remove the foil lid and continue to cook for a further 20 minutes. Remove and discard the garlic, then spoon the pumpkin into a food processor and blend into a purée. Place a fine-mesh sieve over a large bowl (so there is some space between the sieve and the bottom of the bowl), then pour the purée into the sieve. Cover and leave overnight in the refrigerator to allow excess water in the purée to drain out. When you are ready to use the purée, reheat it in the microwave or in a saucepan with a little milk to loosen it. Season to taste and serve hot.

1.5 kg (3 lb 5 oz) pumpkin

1 garlic bulb

5 tbsp extra virgin olive oil

Fine salt and freshly ground black pepper

At the Fish Market

We met a couple in the *bacaro* Alla Vedova who said they were there because they were looking for a restaurant where they could eat good fish. The woman pinched her fingers together and gesticulated in the way Italians do when they are exclaiming about prices. I assumed she meant that they didn't want to pay over the top for fish, but she meant quite the opposite! 'How can you charge so little for the fish!' the woman demanded. 'How could you cook it for that?' To her, the cheap price of fish in some of the restaurants they had seen meant that it must be frozen, and fresh fish is everything to an Italian.

When you make your descent into Venice by plane, you can see the aquaculture in the lagoon where soft shell crabs, sea bass, sea bream and eel are all bred, and so fresh farmed fish and shellfish will always be on offer. Strangely for a city surrounded by water, smoked and dried fish have been on the menu for centuries in Venice too.

Creamy Salt Cod

MAKES AROUND 1 KG (2LB 4 OZ)

Gosh, what a heated argument you can get into when you start discussing how to make the best, most creamy, light, tasty, not too salty, not too garlicky *baccalà mantecato.* Our friend Arianna shared the recipe opposite and it's light and creamy. Small amounts are spread onto crostini or squares of Black and White Polenta (see page 34) and served in every *bacaro* on the streets of Venice. Both *baccalà* and stockfish are air-dried cod, but *baccalà* is salted first. How *baccalà* came to Venice is pretty special, so I must to share the story.

In 1431, Captain Querini and his sailors were on a voyage to bring spices back from Crete to the North Sea. On 25 April they were shipwrecked in a terrible storm and drifted at sea until they reached the Lofoten Islands. The locals made them welcome and introduced them to their food and customs. The men were fishermen and fished for cod during their days. Story has it that they didn't just share their food with the ship's crew but were also happy to share their wives during their long days at sea. Months later only some of the sailors and Captain Querini returned home, while the others decided to stay! Stockfish was brought back to Venice and trade began between Norway and Venice that continues to this day. To bring the fish back to life, almost, soak it in the refrigerator for two days, changing the water at least six times during that period. Taste a little to see if it is still very salty and if it is, keep soaking. When the fish is soft and flexible and tastes pleasantly rather than overpoweringly salty, it's ready for cooking. (If you are using stockfish, all you need to look for is that it is soft rather than salty.)

1 kg (2 lb 4 oz) *baccalà* or stockfish, soaked (see left)

Milk

1 garlic clove, peeled

200–300 ml (7–10 fl oz/scant 1 cup–1 cup) sunflower oil

Fine salt

4 tbsp extra virgin olive oil

2 tbsp parsley, finely chopped

METHOD

Put the fish into a large saucepan and cover it with half milk and half water. If any of the fish are in very large pieces, cut them into manageable sizes. Bring to the boil and then reduce the heat and simmer for 10 minutes. Allow the fish to cool in the liquid. When cool enough to touch, remove the fish from the pan – don't throw away the cooking liquid – and peel off the skin, reserving a quarter of it for later. Pick the flesh away from the bones and into a bowl. Thoroughly check through the flesh to make sure it is bone-free. Cut the reserved skin into tiny shreds with a sharp knife and add to the flesh.

Put the fish into a blender with a whisk attachment, add the garlic, 200 ml (7 fl oz/scant 1 cup) of the cooking liquid and around 100 ml (3 fl oz/scant 1/2 cup) of the sunflower oil. Whisk for around 15 minutes slowing adding more oil in a stream as you would if making mayonnaise. It will begin to look white and fluffy; continue to add the oil until it looks creamy and soft. You may not need all of the oil. Taste and season with salt if necessary and remove the bruised garlic. Finally, drizzle with the olive oil and serve on crostini or polenta with the parsley on top.

VONGOLE ALLO ZENZERO

Clams in Ginger Broth

SERVES 4 AS A STARTER

Fresh ginger is perhaps a new addition to clams in Venice, rather than a continuation of its use since the days of the spice trade, and it may well be as a result of recent Asian inspiration. Restaurant chefs have found that some people don't like to eat garlic, so they think of other flavourings such as chilli or ginger. It is really important to check the clams before using them to make sure they don't contain sand or are already dead. We get our children to drop them one by one into a bowl from a 15 cm (6 in) height and if they have sand in them they will burst open and release the sand. This way you can discard any that do contain sand, any with broken shells or any that are open and don't close with a tap, which means they are dead. You can also make this recipe with cleaned mussels.

METHOD

Heat the oil in a large frying pan with a lid. Add the garlic, ginger and some pepper and fry over a gentle heat for 2 minutes, making sure the garlic and ginger don't burn. Turn up the heat, add the clams and wine and put on the lid. Shake the pan frequently and cook for around 5–7 minutes until all the clams have opened. Discard any that haven't after this time. Toss the parsley through and serve with bread to mop up the juices that are too good to waste.

2 tbsp extra virgin olive oil

2 garlic cloves, finely chopped

2 tbsp fresh ginger, finely chopped

Freshly ground black pepper, to taste

1 kg (2 lb 4 oz) live clams

4 tbsp white wine

1 tbsp parsley, finely chopped

CAPE LONGHE CON AGLIO E PREZZEMOLO

Razor Clams with Garlic and Parsley

At Mascaron, a packed little restaurant in Venice, we drank wine out of small tumblers and ate bowls of razor clams with our fingers served on brown paper squares on wooden tables. Warm bread was on hand in baskets to mop up the delicious juices. This was my first taste of baby razor clams that had been fried in olive oil and garlic. The clam season had just begun and this meant the young clams were ripe for eating. A few weeks into the season they become long and chewy and can only be chopped up and used in a fish stew. I understand now why they are so good to eat, as I had tried to make them in the UK before but we were cooking the clams when they were old and tough. These babies melt in your mouth.

METHOD

Discard any dead or damaged razor clams; if you tap the open clam and it doesn't close, it's dead. Cook following the same method as the Clams in Ginger Broth (see page 182), replacing the clams with razor clams, but omitting the ginger.

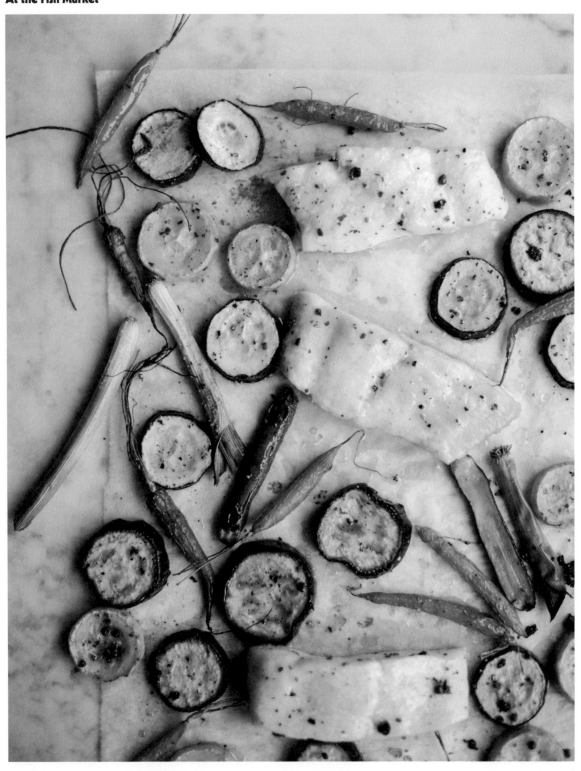

ROMBO CON AGRUMI, TRE PEPE E GINEPRO

Turbot with Three Pepper and Juniper Dressing

SERVES 4

At the restaurants Testiere, Gatto Nero and La Cantina we ate the most simple but perfectly cooked fish with the simplest of accompaniments of vegetables, excellent olive oil and a scattering of herbs and spices. This dish works all year round as turbot is mostly farmed in Italy. We like to use baby vegetables in spring, such as carrots, leek, turnips and spring onions (scallions). In summer, we like to use ripe red (bell) peppers, aubergines (eggplants) and cherry tomatoes, and root vegetables in winter, although they do need a little longer in the oven.

6 tbsp extra virgin olive oil

1 heaped tsp juniper berries, crushed in a pestle and mortar

Fine salt

1 heaped tsp each of 3 types of peppercorns, such as pink, Sichuan, cubeb or long pepper, crushed

4 turbot (or other white fish) fillets, around 150 g (5½ oz) each

Handful of herbs such as parsley, dill, wild fennel, or oregano, finely chopped

FOR THE VEGETABLES, USE A SEASONAL SELECTION OF THE FOLLOWING:

1 aubergine (eggplant), cut into 1 cm (½ in) slices

1 leek, cut into 1 cm (½ in) slices, or 4 baby leeks, left whole

1 fennel bulb, cut lengthways into 1 cm (½ in) slices

8 baby carrots, scrubbed and left whole with a few tops left on

1 red (bell) pepper, seeded and cut lengthways into 8 pieces

1 courgette (zucchini), cut into 1 cm (½ in) slices, or 4 baby courgettes, halved lengthways

METHOD

Preheat the oven to 180°C (350°F/Gas 4). In a bowl mix together 4 tablespoons of the olive oil with the crushed juniper berries, 1 teaspoon each of salt and crushed peppercorns. Lay the vegetables onto a baking tray lined with baking parchment and brush with the spicy oil. Roast for 10–15 minutes or until they are tender.

Meanwhile brush the fish with the rest of the oil, season with salt and put onto the tray with the vegetables. Cook for a further 10 minutes. When the fish is firm to the touch remove from the oven and arrange onto a warmed serving plate with the vegetables. Scatter with the herbs and a splash of your best olive oil.

Eel in Bay Leaves

SERVES 4

This dish is made with eel, which is called *ara* in Venetian dialect, and has been a tradition in Venice for centuries. It is full of spices but retains a delicate flavour that doesn't overwhelm the eel and it has a real wow factor in the presentation. When I ate this at Bistrot de Venise, I began to understand how really exciting it must have been to live in Venice during the 15th and 16th centuries. Surely for many visitors such a variety of exotic flavours, not to mention the sights of Venice, must have been overwhelming for the senses.

The eel is covered with pepper and cooked in bay leaves. It was always cooked slowly at the front of the old ovens. If you can't get hold of sustainably caught eel, we have used mackerel and trout for this and both work equally well.

1 tsp each
of 3 types of
peppercorns, such
as black, pink,
Sichuan, cubeb
or long pepper

30 g (1 oz/2 tbsp)
lard or butter

1 kg (2 lb 4 oz) eel

Around 30
bay leaves

2 tbsp extra
virgin olive oil,
plus extra for
oiling the eel

1½ tbsp fruit
vinegar, such
as raspberry

Fine salt

Few tbsp Fish
Stock (bouillon)
(see page 117)
or hot water

METHOD

Preheat the oven to 70°C (150°F, gas as low as possible). Crush the peppercorns roughly in a pestle and mortar. Lay out 2 sheets of baking paper, one on top of the other, 1 vertical and 1 horizontal, large enough to wrap the eel. Use your fingers to smear the top sheet with lard in a rectangle in the centre, the same width and length of the eel. Lay over the bay leaves, slightly overlapping, so they cover the lard. Add a few drops of oil over the eel and 1 teaspoon of the vinegar. Season the eel inside and out with salt and half of the peppercorns and add the stock or water as well. Roll the eel up in the baking parchment. Twist the ends to secure the eel tightly in the parcel and put onto a baking tray. Bake for 1 hour.

Carefully unroll the eel parcel and pour the juices into a saucepan. Pour in the rest of the vinegar and olive oil and heat through. Add the rest of the peppercorns and season with salt as necessary. Transfer the eel and bay leaves to a warm flat plate to serve, discarding the baking paper. Pour over the juices and serve.

BRANZINO CON VONGOLE E FAGIOLI DI LAMON

Sea Bass and Clams on Lamon Beans

SERVES 4

We ate this at the perfect little restaurant, Carampane, in the area near Rialto. Francesco and his staff make you feel very welcome, despite the sign on the door saying 'No tourist menu, no pizza and no pasta'. He takes his food very seriously and rightly so. My fish was so fresh and perfectly cooked it was weeping lagoon water as I ate it. We loved the sea bass on velvety smooth beans. Francesco likes to use the smooth, creamy gialet beans, which are a Slow Food Organisation approved product, grown in Lamon, Belluna, just north of Venice. Bring some back in your suitcase or use haricot (navy) or cannellini instead. If time permits, use dried beans, soaked overnight, or see my tips for cooking beans on page 145. If time is very short, a tin of beans will do.

200 g (7 oz/1 cup) dried gialet or cannellini beans, or similar, soaked

1 shallot

1 bay leaf

Fine salt and freshly ground black pepper

6 tbsp extra virgin olive oil

20 cherry tomatoes, halved

3 sprigs of thyme

1 garlic clove, whole, lightly crushed

300 g (10½ oz) fresh clams, washed and checked for sand (see page 182)

2 tbsp white wine

4 sea bass fillets

100 g (3½ oz/ 1 cup) fine dry breadcrumbs (see page 24)

1 tbsp parsley, roughly chopped, leaves and stalks

METHOD

Put the soaked beans into a heavy-based saucepan with a lid. Add the shallot and bay leaf and cover with water 5 cm (2 in) deep on top of the beans. Bring to the boil and boil rapidly for 10 minutes. Reduce the heat and simmer for 1 hour until they are tender. (See pages 144–5 to read more on cooking beans.) Drain and transfer one-third of the beans to a blender. Purée them and then mix back into the pan. Season to taste and add 1 tablespoon of the olive oil. Cover and keep the mixture warm.

Put the tomatoes onto a grill (broiler) pan, season and sprinkle over the thyme leaves. Grill for 10 minutes or until lightly browned and soft. Set aside.

Heat 2 tablespoons of the oil in a large saucepan with a lid, add the garlic and fry for 1 minute, add the clams and wine. Put on the lid and shake the pan frequently. Cook for just a few minutes until the clams have all opened. Discard any that haven't. Pick out most of the clams from the shells and put them back into the cooking liquor, keeping aside a few whole for garnish.

Season the fish and dip them into the breadcrumbs, tap off the excess. Heat the remaining oil in a large non-stick frying pan and fry the fish, skin down first, for around 3–4 minutes, then turn to the other side and fry for a further 2–3 minutes or until golden brown on both sides.

To serve, pour the warm beans into warm shallow bowls, top with the fish and scatter over a few clams, a little cooking liquor, the cherry tomatoes and parsley.

SOGLIOLA IN PADELLA
Pan-fried Dover Sole

SERVES 2

Trattoria La Madonna does pan-fried sole so well that I went there for lunch with my friend Juliet only to go back in the evening so she could eat it again. The sole had the lightest dusting of flour, then it was quickly fried and served simply with lemon. Dover sole is usually gutted as it is landed but do wash it well and make sure there is no remaining blood inside. Dover sole is a flat fish whose skin is a grey-brown colour on the top side and creamy coloured on the underside. It is usually cooked with the darker top skin removed but the bottom skin left on, so ask your fishmonger to remove the grey skin for you or do it yourself. Make a shallow cut through the grey skin just above the tail and pull it away from tail to head using a cloth to grip the skin tightly while holding the tail with the other hand.

2 x 250 g (9 oz) Dover sole, grey skin removed

Salt and freshly ground black pepper

60 g (2 oz/½ cup) '00' or plain (all-purpose) flour

3 tbsp olive oil

1 garlic clove, whole, lightly crushed

50 g (1¾ oz/ ½ stick) salted butter

Juice of 1 small lemon

1 tbsp parsley, finely chopped

METHOD

Preheat the oven to 180°C (350°F/Gas 4). Season the fish and dip them into a bowl containing the flour. Pat the fish to get rid of the excess; this is really important so that the fish only have the lightest covering of flour. Heat the oil and garlic clove in a large frying pan over a medium heat. When the oil just starts to smell of garlic, add the fish and brown the skinless side only, around 2 minutes should do it. Transfer the fish to a baking tray lined with baking parchment and put into the oven for 12–15 minutes until cooked. To test for this, use a dinner knife and push it between the spine and the flesh. If the flesh twists away easily from the spine, the fish is cooked.

Meanwhile, melt the butter in a saucepan, then add the lemon juice and parsley and shake to combine. Add 1 tablespoon of water and shake again. Put the fish onto a warm plate and serve with the sauce.

GRIGLIATA DI PESCE

Seafood on the Grill

SERVES 4 AS A MAIN OR 6 AS A STARTER

As the seafood is so fresh in Venice, little needs to be done to it. Crisp baby squid, sardines, cuttlefish and tuna are grilled (broiled) very briefly and served up anointed with green olive oil before being served to the awaiting customers. This is the way our head chef Gregorio Piazza grills fish. He uses a griddle pan to get the flavour and black lines on the seafood and then finishes cooking it in the oven. Marinating is great for infusing flavour into fish. As the seafood will cook quickly, have everything ready to go before you start. The thinnest seafood will take the least amount of time. Calamari and fish will become opaque and firm to the touch when done. Thicker fish such as tuna and stone bass will take a few minutes longer but will also be firm to the touch when cooked through.

1 kg (2 lb 4 oz) seafood, such as fillets of mackerel, sole, stone bass, prawns (shrimp) in their shells, squid

Finely grated zest and juice of ½ lemon

Finely grated zest and juice of ½ orange

Few parsley stalks, crushed in a pestle and mortar

Few sprigs of thyme

Fine salt

3 tbsp extra virgin olive oil, green is ideal, plus extra to serve

Small handful of parsley leaves, roughly chopped, to serve

METHOD

If using squid, open them up and make criss-crosses lightly in one side of the flesh, cut into pieces around 5 cm (2 in) wide (baby ones can be left whole, if preferred). Mix together the lemon and orange zests and juices, parsley stalks, thyme, salt and olive oil. Lay all the seafood in a shallow dish and pour over the marinade. Cover and leave in the refrigerator for 15 minutes.

Heat a barbecue, hotplate or a large griddle pan over a high heat and, when it's really hot, lay the seafood onto it, starting with the thickest pieces first and putting on the quickest cooking seafood last; fish should be laid skin-side down. When each piece is done on one side, turn over and cook the other side. The squid will only take 1 minute or so, the prawns (unless they are large and have shells on) will also be quick, but ensure you cook them until completely pink. Leave the fish until just over half of it has become opaque, then turn and cook briefly on the other side. White fish fillets will take around 5 minutes in total and a salmon steak will take 8–10 minutes. For rare tuna, cook for just 1–2 minutes on each side. Set the fish aside as it is done on a warmed serving dish. Serve drizzled with olive oil and sprinkled with the parsley.

SEPPIE NERE

Black Cuttlefish

SERVES 4

I love this unusual and dramatic dish. I ate this with my friend Juliet at La Madonna. She grimaced at my black cuttlefish as I grinned at her with blackened teeth! Cleaning cuttlefish is not quick and is messy, so buy them ready prepared from the fishmonger unless you want black splashes over your kitchen and clothes. Also ask for a couple of the ink sacs if they can isolate them for you. You will need this for the sauce. Alternatively, buy cuttlefish ink from a fishmonger, online or at an Italian deli.

METHOD

Heat the butter and oil together in a large frying pan with a lid and, when hot, fry the onion and garlic over a low heat until soft. Add the cuttlefish and cook stirring frequently for 15 minutes. Pour in the brandy and ink. Allow the strong smell of brandy to dissipate for 4–5 minutes, then put the lid on the pan and leave to cook over a low heat. Test a piece of cuttlefish after 45 minutes and if it is still chewy, continue to cook until tender. Season, sprinkle with parsley and serve with soft polenta (see page 111).

50 g (1¾ oz/ ½ stick) salted butter

3 tbsp extra virgin olive oil

1 large white onion, finely chopped

2 garlic cloves, lightly crushed

800 g (1 lb 12 oz) cuttlefish, cleaned and cut into bite-size pieces, ink sacs reserved or 2 tbsp good-quality cuttlefish ink

100 ml (3½ fl oz/ scant ½ cup) brandy

Salt and freshly ground black pepper

Handful of flat-leaf parsley, roughly chopped

GAMBERI CROCCANTI CON ZUCCA IN SAOR

Crispy Prawns on Sweet and Sour Pumpkin

SERVES 4

This stunning dish was shot at L'Osteria di Santa Marina. We loved the idea of crunchy prawns (shrimp) on sweet and sour pumpkin and the pumpkin purée is really a puréed pumpkin risotto. The kataifi pastry can be ordered online or bought in some Greek shops. It's fun to use and looks amazing.

FOR THE PUMPKIN PURÉE

1 shallot or small white onion, finely chopped

2 tbsp extra virgin olive oil, plus extra to serve

30 g (1 oz/2 tbsp) butter

400 g (14 oz) pumpkin or butternut squash, peeled and diced into 2 cm (¾ in) cubes

30 g (1 oz/2 tbsp) arborio or other risotto rice

25 ml (1 fl oz) white wine

200 ml (7 fl oz/ scant 1 cup) Vegetable Stock (bouillon) (see page 115)

30 g (1 oz) Parmesan, finely grated

Salt and freshly ground black pepper

FOR THE PRAWNS

1 quantity of Pumpkin in Saor (see page 177)

1 litre (34 fl oz/ 4¼ cups) sunflower oil for deep-frying

400 g (14 oz) kataifi pastry

Few sprigs of thyme

12 prawns (shrimp)

METHOD

Sweat the onions in a large frying pan in the oil and butter over a low heat until soft. Add the pumpkin to the pan and continue to cook for 5 minutes. Pour in the rice and wine and stir through for 2 minutes. Add the stock and continue to cook over a medium heat, stirring frequently, particularly towards the end of the cooking time. When most of the water has disappeared, check that the pumpkin and rice are soft; if not, add a little more water and continue to cook. It should take around 30–40 minutes. Remove from the heat, add the Parmesan and purée with a hand-held blender or food processor. Season to taste.

Reheat the pumpkin in saor in a medium saucepan covered with a lid, stirring occasionally.

Heat the sunflower oil in a high-sided pan until it is hot enough to make a breadcrumb sizzle when dropped in. Unroll the pastry and tear away pieces large enough to wind round the prawns. Scatter the thyme leaves onto a plate. Season the prawns, press them into the thyme leaves and wrap each of the prawns in a little of the pastry. Carefully fry in the hot oil for around 1–2 minutes until golden brown and the prawns are cooked through. Remove and drain on some paper towels.

Spread a little of the pumpkin purée onto a plate, top with 3 rounds of pumpkins in saor, using a ring mould or pastry cutter to shape them. Lay a crisply fried prawn on each. Drizzle with olive oil and serve straight away.

At the Butchers

Most meat is brought into Venice by boat from mainland Italy. And though fish-based menus are everywhere, meat is plentiful in restaurants such as La Taverna La Fenice where they specialise in carnivorous fare, including *fegato alla veneziana* – calves' liver and onions.

Goose and duck were first made fashionable by Jewish settlers, small waterfowl from the lagoon have always been popular, and, perhaps surprisingly, you will find turkey mentioned in many recipe books, often served with a pomegranate sauce.

On 21 November every year, the day of Madonna della Salute, *castradina* (smoked mutton) is eaten with cabbage soup. If you are visiting Venice at this time, you will see the legs of lamb hanging in butchers that have been brought in for this celebration.

Cotechino and the similar musetto are large cured pork sausages sold in delis, which are boiled and usually served with mustard or horseradish and polenta.

SELVAGGINA IN UMIDO

Pot Roast Game in Wine

SERVES 6

Francesco at restaurant La Cantina wanted to show us his way of cooking pigeon, unfortunately he had none in the refrigerator. As he began to eye up one in the street, the butcher arrived in the nick of time with a large quail and the street pigeon got to live another day! If you have ever roasted pheasant, partridge, rabbit, duck or quail and found it dry, then you will know why I am more than happy to pot roast every time. Basically birds are not designed to be roasted. Their tough legs have higher collagen levels than their breasts, so they need longer cooking. But if you get the legs right, you have probably overcooked the breast and, conversely, if the breast is juicy, the legs are pink and tough. The answer? Joint the bird and cook the pieces separately or pot roast slowly until the meat falls from the bones. Italian sausages have a great flavour as they contain garlic, wine and no bread. If you omit them, add a couple of garlic cloves instead.

GUEST RECIPE Francesco

2 pheasants,
1 duck,
4 partridges
or 6 quails

Fine salt and
freshly ground
black pepper

6 rashers (slices)
of unsmoked
bacon

1–6 sprigs of
thyme (1 per bird)

30 g (1 oz/2 tbsp)
salted butter

3 tbsp extra
virgin olive oil

2 best-quality
Italian or pork
sausages
(optional)

1 white onion,
roughly chopped

2 short sprigs
of rosemary

1 bay leaf

200 ml (7 fl oz/
scant 1 cup) white
or Madeira wine
(or half and half)

100–200 ml
(3½–7 fl oz/scant
½ cup) Vegetable
or Chicken stock
(bouillon) (see
pages 115–116)
or water

**COOKING TIMES
FOR THE BIRDS**

Quails –
around 1 hour

Partridges –
1½ hours

Pheasants –
1¾–2 hours

Duck –
2 hours

METHOD

Preheat the oven to 160°C (325°F/Gas 3). Season the birds generously and wrap them in the bacon, enclosing 1 sprig of thyme with each one. Secure with string or a toothpick. (If you find this challenging or are not going to serve the birds whole, simply cut the rashers into quarters and put them in the pot with the thyme.) On the hob, melt the butter and oil together in a flameproof casserole (one that has a lid) and brown the birds and sausages until golden all over. Add the onions, rosemary and bay leaf. When the onions have softened, pour in the wine and let it bubble for a couple of minutes. Add the stock, put on the lid and transfer to the oven. Cook for the times stated opposite or until the meat falls from the bones easily.

Remove from the oven and check the level of liquid. Serve the birds straight away with the sauce (spoon off excess fat first) if you are happy with the taste and consistency. If you have a lot of liquid, remove and rest the birds in a warm place covered with foil, then reduce the sauce over the heat on the hob, strain and serve.

For a fatty bird like duck, spoon away the oil first and reduce the sauce. If you are cooking the birds to put into the Good Game Pie, remove the birds and keep the sauce following the instructions on page 65. Serve with soft polenta (see page 111) and the strained juices from the casserole.

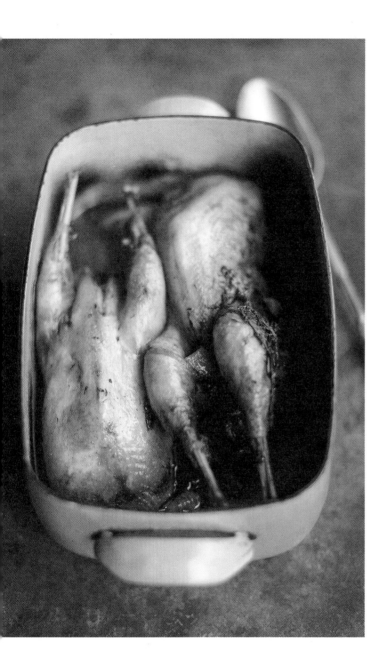

Francesco loves to pair different small bites to go with the quail, almost like *cicchetti* on the plate. In the photograph on page 110, you can see chargrilled leek, black and yellow potatoes, toasted polenta, porcini mushrooms, horseradish sauce, soft and crumbly goat's cheese, sage leaves and red rice. We love to eat Pot Roast meat with the Garlic Sauce for Meat on page 219.

Game ragù for pasta: pick all the meat from the bones and put it back into the pot with the sauce, heat though and stir into Potato Gnocchi (see page 101) or short pasta.

SALSA DI MELOGRANO E ZENZERO ALLA PERFEZIONE

Perfect and Quick Pomegranate and Ginger Sauce

SERVES 4–6

Pomegranate trees are a common sight over Italy and yet you hardly ever see the ruby red seeds used in cooking nowadays. However, they were commonly used in the past and their jewel-like qualities were gloriously depicted in famous paintings. They are also often portrayed as a symbol of fertility due to their many seeds. If you have a glut of pomegranates, by all means remove the seeds and crush them. However, if time is short and pressed pomegranate juice is available at your local supermarket, buy it and be happy. You really won't notice much difference; I have tried it on your behalf. The idea for this came from the medieval chef the Anonimo Veneziano's recipe below:

'Good relish for chickens. To give a good flavour to chickens. Take pomegranates and squeeze out the juice. Put into the pomegranate juice good sweet spices. If it seems too strong, mix dill/anise ground, or rose water. Alternatively use the juice of grated sour apples and juice of good sweet grapes mixed together with enough sweet spices. If you do not have grapes put in a little honey and let it boil. The spices should taste raw, not cooked, don't allow it to cook too much or the sauce will spoil.'

Juice of 4 pomegranates (seeds bashed out and squeezed) or 300 ml (10 fl oz/ 1¼ cups) pomegranate juice

2 tsp mild clear honey

2 tsp sugar

Pinch of salt

10 g (½ oz) fresh ginger, finely grated

2 cloves

Small cinnamon stick

2–4 heaped tsp cornflour (cornstarch)

METHOD

Heat the juice, honey, sugar, salt, ginger, cloves and cinnamon together in a saucepan and bring to the boil. Turn down the heat and let it simmer for 5 minutes. For a runny gravy, you need just 2 teaspoons of cornflour and for a relish you will need 4 teaspoons. Mix the cornflour with enough cold water to make a paste and then pour into warm mixture. Bring to the boil and cook for at least 1 minute, or until it thickens to the consistency you want. Remove from the heat and serve. The sauce or relish will keep, covered, in the refrigerator for around 4 days. Serve at room temperature.

LE SECOE CON SPUMA DI PATATE

Rich Beef Stew with Parmesan Mash

SERVES 6 AS A MAIN OR 10 AS A STARTER

In Ristorante Taverna La Fenice, which has to be one of the prettiest and most romantic places in Venice, they serve an ancient recipe for slowly cooking the meat from the spine of beef called *le secoe*. This dish is totally delicious: a cloud of cheesy potato on a rich beef stew. Traditionally this is eaten with risotto but here the chef served it in the bottom of a martini glass and topped it with foamed mashed potato which had Parmesan in it. The restaurant has served mainly meat dishes, as an alternative to the mainly fish restaurants, to opera singers and enthusiasts from the opera house, Teatro La Fenice, for generations; Maria Callas was a regular. There is even a secret passage connecting the restaurant to the theatre for the use of the artists.

It is hard to buy spine these days but really any cut that will break down slowly is ideal. So cheaper cuts of beef that we should be making more of are perfect for this dish. We have used beef neck, and sometimes beef cheeks, both of which render a rich flavour and soft meat after a few hours in the oven.

FOR THE *SECOE*

1.25 kg (2 lb 12 oz) beef neck on the bone or 1 kg (2 lb 4 oz) beef cheeks, trimmed of sinew or stewing steak

Fine salt and freshly ground black pepper

4 tbsp extra virgin olive oil

30 g (1 oz/2 tbsp) salted butter

1 large white onion, finely chopped

1 celery stalk, roughly chopped

1 carrot, roughly chopped

1 long sprig of rosemary

120 ml (4 fl oz/ ½ cup) white wine

1 litre (34 fl oz/ 4¼ cups) beef, Vegetable or Chicken stock (bouillon) (see pages 115–116)

FOR THE POTATO MASH

2 kg (4 lb 8 oz) floury potatoes

100 g (3½ oz) Parmesan, finely grated

200 ml (7 fl oz/ scant 1 cup) double (heavy) cream

200 ml (7 fl oz/ scant 1 cup) milk

100 g (3½ oz/ scant ½ cup) salted butter

1 tsp fine salt

METHOD

Pre-heat the oven to 160°C (325°F/ Gas 3). Season the beef and put it into a casserole dish over a medium– high heat with the olive oil, butter, vegetables and rosemary. Lightly brown the meat on all sides and then add the wine. Pour in the stock. Bring to the boil, cover with a lid and transfer to the oven.

Cook for up to 4 hours or until the meat falls from the bones. If you are using a different cut of beef, the cooking time will differ, for example stewing steak may only take 1½ hours. Whatever cut you use, the meat should be cooked until it is really meltingly soft. Allow to cool. Spoon off the fat from the top of the stew and discard. Pick the meat off the bones if there are any and put the meat back into the sauce. Discard the bones.

Cook the potatoes whole in their skins. This gives a better flavour and stops them from becoming saturated with water and making the mash soggy. Drain and allow to cool for a few minutes, then peel them using a fork to hold the potato and a knife to help peel away the skin. Mash them through a ricer or food mill into a large bowl with the Parmesan, cream, milk, butter and salt. Use an electric beater to whisk in air and lightness, this will also help to get rid of any lumps so that the mash is completely smooth. To serve this as a starter, reheat the stew and divide into 10 small dishes. If you have a whipping siphon, use this to pipe the foamy mash onto the hot stew. If you don't, carefully spoon the mash on top instead. For a main course, serve the stew onto piles of creamy mash. Any leftovers are wonderful on pasta or soft polenta with plenty of grated Parmesan.

FEGATO ALLA VENEZIANA

Venetian Liver and Onions

SERVES 4

When done properly this is about as far away as you can get from school dinners. It is the most popular meat on our menu and always has been. I think this is because people don't like to prepare it at home, but instead they want to enjoy it in a restaurant. Giancarlo loves it and the best version he ate in Venice was at Harry's Bar, so here he is going to tell you exactly how to make it based on their recipe.

Arrigo Cipriani, Harry's Bar's owner, told us that the preparation of this dish is as important as the cooking. The liver should be thoroughly cleaned of all membrane and any sinew. It is then sliced thinly with a razor-sharp knife so that after cooking each piece just melts in your mouth.

3 medium white onions, cut into fine half-moons (see page 46)

6 tbsp extra virgin olive oil

900 g (2 lb) calves' livers, sliced into strips 5 mm (¼ in) thick and 4–5 cm (2 in) wide

Fine salt and freshly ground black pepper

30 g (1 oz/2 tbsp) salted butter

METHOD

Fry the onions over a low heat in a pan with 4 tablespoons of the olive oil for about 25 minutes until soft and lightly browned. Remove the onions using tongs to reserve the oil in the pan. Set the onions aside on a warmed dish.

Turn up the heat, add the rest of the oil and fry the liver for 2–4 minutes maximum; just until it loses its colour. Add the onions back to the pan, season and toss through. Pour onto a warmed serving dish. Add the butter to the pan and mix in any brown bits from bottom. Pour the butter sauce over the liver and serve straight away with soft polenta, toasted set polenta (see page 111) or mashed potatoes.

PETTO D'ANATRA CON PEVERADA E MELE SPEZIATE

Duck Breasts with Peverada Sauce and Spiced Apple Compote

SERVES 6–8

This medieval recipe is still made in Venice today. This may seem a complex recipe but it can be made in advance. Any bird can be used, the idea being the sauce is made from the liver. This version is from chef Mario from Bistrot de Venise. Any leftover sauce is wonderful with hot pasta, soft polenta or crostini.

METHOD

To prepare the duck breasts, score the skin all over in a criss-cross pattern, season and press on the chopped vegetables so they cover the breasts. Put the duck into a vacuum, sous-vide or roasting bag suitable for cooking at low temperatures in the oven. Squeeze out the air and seal the bag or use a vacuum machine. Refrigerate for 8 hours or overnight. Preheat the oven to 70°C (150°F, gas as low as possible) and cook the duck in the plastic bag for 1 hour.

To make the *peverada* sauce, lay the livers onto paper towels for a few minutes to dry them out. Put the lemon juice into a saucepan over a medium heat and allow it to bubble away until it is reduced by half. In a separate pan, sweat the onion in the oil over a low heat with salt and a generous amount of pepper for around 10 minutes until translucent. Blitz the sausages into a fine mince in a food processor, then scrape into a bowl. Do the same for the

salami; this is done separately as the meats break up differently. Add both minced meats to the onion and brown all over. Take off the heat.

Trim away the white connective tissue between the livers and discard. Using a large cook's knife, chop the livers into a coarse mince. This is best not done in a food processor as it turns to paste. Remove and discard the excess oil from the saucepan containing the browned sausage meat. Do this by resting the saucepan on a chopping board so that it tips to one side and pull the mince over to the higher side with a wooden spoon. The oil will collect in lower side. Spoon this out and discard. Put back over a low heat and add the chopped livers. Simmer the mixture slowly over a low heat for around 30 minutes until browned and dry. It is important that it is dry as the liquid from the livers can be bitter if left.

Add the gherkins, garlic, lemon juice and stock and bring to the boil,

then turn down the heat to simmer for around 30 minutes. Add the icing sugar and adjust the seasoning as necessary, remembering that it should have a definite kick of pepper. The sauce can be made a day or two in advance and kept, covered, in the refrigerator.

To make the apple compote, put the onion and sugar together in a small saucepan. Cook for 5 minutes over a medium heat. Add the apples and mustard powder and cook for a further 5 minutes until the apple becomes golden. Add the pine nuts and sultanas, pour in the vinegar and wine and cook for another 5 minutes. Serve at room temperature.

Fry the duck, skin-down in a non-stick frying pan over a low heat for 10 minutes, then turn to the flesh side and cook for 5 minutes. Reheat the *peverada* sauce in a frying pan, pour onto warmed plates, top with the duck and serve with the apple compote.

FOR THE DUCK BREASTS

6–8 duck breasts

Salt and freshly ground black pepper

1 celery stalk, finely chopped

½ onion, finely chopped

1 small carrot, finely chopped

1 sprig of rosemary, leaves picked

FOR THE APPLE COMPOTE

200 g (7 oz) onion, roughly chopped

100 g (3½ oz/ scant ½ cup) Demerara sugar

400 g (14 oz) apples, peeled, cored and cut into 2 cm (¾ in) cubes

½ tsp mustard powder

50 g (1¾ oz) pine nuts

50 g (1¾ oz/⅓ cup) sultanas (golden raisins)

3 tbsp white wine vinegar

4 tbsp white wine

FOR THE *PEVERADA* SAUCE

500 g (1 lb 2 oz) chicken livers

Juice of 2 lemons

1 medium white onion, finely chopped

3 tbsp extra virgin olive oil

Fine salt and freshly ground black pepper

150 g (5½ oz) sausages

200 g (7 oz) salami

6 mini gherkins, finely chopped

1 medium garlic clove, finely chopped

750 ml (25 fl oz/ 3 cups) chicken stock (bouillon) (see page 116)

1 tbsp icing (powdered) sugar

ROTOLO DI TACCHINO CON ASIAGO E SPECK

Turkey stuffed with Asiago Cheese and Speck

SERVES 6

Having dinner with my two Venetian friends Monica and Arianna and ever on the scout for new recipes, I couldn't resist the opportunity to ask them what they cooked at home. Both of them recommended this one, saying it was inexpensive, not lengthy to prepare and all of their family loved it. I gave it a try and it worked on mine too, even fussy children tucked in and asked for more. Speck is made in the Dolomites, the mountains north of Venice. It is a lightly smoked ham that is delicious on its own or in cooking.

METHOD

Remove the bone from the turkey breast and butterfly it. To do this, lay the breast down flat on a chopping board. Place your hand flat over the meat to keep it steady while you cut. Holding the knife with the blade facing sideways, slice down one side of the breast, cutting across widthways and nearly through to the other side. Open up into one big thinner piece, like a book. Season and lay over the slices of speck, asiago and sage leaves. Roll it up and secure tightly with kitchen string, then season. Pour the flour onto a plate and roll the turkey in it so that it is lightly covered all over.

Warm the oil and butter in a large, heavy-based flameproof casserole dish with a lid and add the garlic and turkey breast and brown all over. Add the wine and let it reduce for 4–5 minutes. Add the stock and bring to the boil. Reduce the heat, cover and simmer for about 1 hour or until cooked through (when the turkey reaches 70°C/150°F for at least 2 minutes on a meat thermometer pushed into the centre or the juices run clear when pierced with a skewer). Remove the turkey from the pot and set to rest on a warmed platter covered with foil and a cloth. If there is a lot of sauce in the casserole, reduce it by bubbling it over the heat. If you prefer it thicker, mix 1–2 teaspoons of cornflour with 1 tablespoon of water and add to the sauce. Serve straight away or Monica's tip is to let it cool completely and then cut into slices. Preheat the oven to 180°C (350°F/Gas 4), lay the slices in a baking dish, pour over the sauce, cover with foil and then reheat for around 30 minutes until piping hot.

1 kg (2 lb 4 oz) turkey breast

Fine salt and freshly ground black pepper

100 g (3½ oz) speck ham or smoked bacon

100 g asiago, Comté or Cheddar, cut into 5 mm (¼ in) slices

10 large sage leaves

3 tbsp '00' or plain (all-purpose) flour

4 tbsp extra virgin olive oil

30 g (1 oz/2 tbsp) salted butter

2 garlic gloves, lightly crushed

150 ml (5 fl oz/ ⅔ cup) white wine

150 ml (5 fl oz/ ⅔ cup) Vegetable or Chicken Stock (bouillon) (see pages 115–116) or water

Cornflour (cornstarch), as necessary

AGLIATA PER CARNE

Garlic Sauce for Meat

SERVES 6–8

This wonderful concoction reminds me of the garlic sauce served in Middle Eastern restaurants that I love over roast chicken and also of English bread sauce. It is inspired by a recipe from the 15th century cook Maestro Martino, and adapted by Bistrot de Venise. It is wonderful with Pot Roast Game in Wine (see page 206).

METHOD

Put the garlic clove into a saucepan with water to cover and bring to the boil. Simmer for 2 minutes. Discard the water, cover the garlic with the milk, add the star anise, salt, saffron and ginger, and bring to the boil again. Lower the heat to simmer, remove the garlic cloves with a slotted spoon and put into a food processor with the bread. Blitz into breadcrumbs. Put this mixture back into the pan with the ground almonds. Cook for around 10 minutes until thickened. Remove from the heat and stir in the ricotta. Taste and adjust the spices accordingly. Serve warm with roast meats, poultry and vegetables.

10 garlic cloves, peeled

200 ml (7 fl oz/ scant 1 cup) milk

2 star anise

½ tsp fine salt

½ tsp saffron strands

2 tsp grated fresh ginger

50 g (1¾ oz/ ½ cup) soft bread

50 g (1¾ oz/½ cup) ground almonds

100 g (3½ oz/ ⅓ cup) ricotta

Chicken with Ginger, Saffron and Dates

SERVES 6

Chicken was used a great deal in Italy during the Middle Ages but less so these days. Italians generally seem to prefer the flavour of guinea fowl or game. I love to use it and so I was happy to discover this quick chicken stew among the 14th century recipes written by anonymous chef the Anonimo Veneziana.

'LXXVI. A most perfect quick stew. If you want to make a quick stew. Take six hens and fry them in lard, then take away the lard so that there is not too much. Add (to the pan and the hens) almond milk tempered with verjuice, minutely chopped ginger, dates cut into quarters and to add colour to this dish saffron and it will be a good dish.'

Ingredients

Salt and freshly ground black pepper

1 medium chicken, jointed, or 6 chicken thighs

4 tbsp sunflower oil

100 g (3½ oz) fresh ginger

3 garlic cloves

3 tbsp extra virgin olive oil

1 knob of salted butter

1 large white onion, finely chopped

2 bay leaves

3 cm (1¼ in) cinnamon stick

4 cloves

650 ml (22 fl oz/ 2¾ cups) homemade Almond Milk (page 222) or shop-bought unsweetened almond milk with 50 g (1¾ oz/½ cup) ground almonds

10 medjool dates, stoned and quartered

½ tsp saffron strands

Small bunch of parsley or coriander (cilantro) to serve (optional)

A handful of flaked (slivered), toasted almonds

METHOD

Season the chicken all over, then brown all over in a large frying pan in sunflower oil over a medium heat. Peel the ginger and garlic, then pulse together in a food processor until puréed. Alternatively, finely grate the ginger and garlic into a bowl.

When the chicken is crispy and mid-golden all round, remove from the pan and set aside. Discard the oil.

In a large frying pan that has a lid, warm the olive oil and butter together over a medium heat. Fry the onion for around 5 minutes until just becoming soft. Add the ginger and garlic purée, bay leaves, cinnamon and cloves. Transfer the chicken pieces into the pan and stir through to coat the chicken in the spices. Pour over the almond milk (and ground almonds if using), add the dates and scatter over the strands of saffron.

Once the milk has come to the boil, turn down the heat and cook for 50 minutes to 1 hour with the lid on, or until the meat is falling from the bone. Taste and adjust the seasoning as necessary.

Either serve straight away or allow the chicken to cool and pull the meat from the bones with your fingers. Discard the bones and put the meat back into the sauce and reheat when you are ready to serve. I must admit I prefer it this way as it is easier for people to eat. Decorate the plate with torn parsley or coriander, if using, and the toasted almonds. Serve with rice, the Spiced Cauliflower or Broccoli with Raisins (see page 164) and Buttered Carrots with Herbs (see page 167).

LATTE DI MANDORLE

Almond Milk

MAKES APPROX. 400 ML

The mainstay of many a medieval recipe was nuts, especially almonds, which were ground and used to thicken sauces, or made into white almond milk. In the Strada Nuova is a large nut stand. Here you can find almonds jostling with wonderful wet walnuts, pistachios and caramel-coloured hazelnuts.

Almond milk was a staple ingredient in the medieval Venetian kitchen. It was made then more or less as it can be made now, except that my sieve is metal rather than made from horsehair! We have used this almond milk in the Chicken with Ginger, Saffron and Dates (see page 221), and the Almond Milk Rice Pudding with Cardamom and Orange (see page 244). Shop-bought almond milk is fine to use as a replacement, I would go for unsweetened in both cases. This same method can be followed to make hazelnut or cashew milk.

METHOD

To make almond milk, take 100 g (3½ oz) shelled but not peeled almonds and soak in enough cold water to cover them for 8 hours to 2 days in the refrigerator; change the water twice during this time. (Shelled almonds with skins give more flavour than blanched almonds but either can be used.) The longer you leave them, the more flavour you get. Strain, discard the water and put the nuts into a food processor with 400 ml (13 fl oz/generous 1½ cups) of clean water. Blend until finely ground and you have a creamy milk. Pour into a large lidded jug or bowl, cover and store in the refrigerator for up to 3 days. This will give you a mild flavour and thickish milk. If you don't want the bits or you want a thinner milk, you can strain it but I like to keep them in. If you do sieve it, the almond meal can be dried in a very low oven and used in any recipe that calls for ground almonds.

POLASTI AFENOCHIATAI VANTAZATI

Fantastic Chicken with Fennel and Fine Spices

SERVES 4

This might seem like an odd title but it was the name given by medieval chef the Anonimo Veneziano who wrote *Libro per Cuoco*, a collection of Venetian dishes. He was obviously pretty impressed by his own recipes. With a little help from our friend and spice queen Manjula Samarasinghe we were able to use the typical spices from medieval Venice, such as fennel seeds and saffron, to create this dish, which is well worth its title. Anonimo Veneziano adds egg yolks to thicken the sauce like a fricassee and saffron to give it colour. He used lardo, the seasoned and cured back fat of pork, which, if you can find it, is delicious. Failing that, sunflower oil, as we have used here, is perfectly acceptable.

8 skinless chicken thighs

1 tsp salt

2 tsp freshly ground black pepper

2 tsp white wine vinegar

15 g (½ oz) fresh ginger, grated or minced in a food processor

2 garlic cloves, grated or minced in a food processor

2 tsp fennel seeds

1 medium onion, finely chopped

3 tbsp sunflower oil

1 fennel bulb, roughly chopped and green fronds reserved if there are any

½ tsp saffron strands

400 ml (14 fl oz/ generous 1½ cups) Vegetable or Chicken stock (bouillon) (see page 115–116) or water

2 egg yolks, beaten

1 tbsp lemon juice

METHOD

Put the chicken thighs, salt, pepper, vinegar, ginger and garlic into a clean plastic bag and refrigerate for 30 minutes or up to overnight.

Dry-fry the fennel seeds in a small frying pan. As they become fragrant and turn golden, remove them from the heat and pour onto a plate to cool. Grind 1 teaspoon of them in a pestle and mortar or spice blender, reserving the rest whole for later.

Put the onion into a large frying pan that has a lid and fry gently in the sunflower oil over a low heat until soft. Add the chicken with the marinade, chopped fennel, ground fennel seeds, saffron and stock, bring to the boil and then turn the heat to medium. Scatter over the remaining whole seeds. Cover and cook the chicken until it falls from the bones, around 45 minutes.

Mix the egg yolks with the lemon juice in a small bowl. Push the chicken to one side of the pan so the juices gather in a pool. Pour in the yolk and lemon, stirring through quickly to thicken the sauce. Do not allow to boil. Serve with rice or bread and the Buttered Carrots with Herbs (see page 167).

At the Patisserie

Walking the narrow streets of Venice you come across so many tempting displays of cakes, biscuits, candied fruits and chocolate. During *carnevale* do try the *frittelle* and *galani* which are crisp pastries dusted with icing (powdered) sugar. Fried and sugared goodies are ubiquitous in old and modern Venice – fried pear and apple slices and elderflowers (picked early in the morning) were popular street food in the Renaissance. They can be battered and fried using the simple batter recipe on page 226.

Do bring back a decorative tin of baicoli biscuits, they are perfect for dunking in zabaglione cream or a glass of Madeira. Look out for the Austrian influence in the pastries and the sachertorte, deliciously rich chocolate cakes sold in most patisseries. Traditional Venetian cakes are the *pincia*, a spiced bread pudding, and the focaccia, which here means a sweet, light sponge.

FRITTELLE DELL'IMPERATORE CON SALSA DI CILIEGIE

Almond-filled Doughnuts with Cherry Coulis

SERVES 12 (MAKES 36 FRITTELLE)

'Feed me these on a daily basis and I will be yours forever.' A bit over the top perhaps but that is how I felt eating these gorgeous filled doughnuts and it is what I said to Giancarlo before he went to work at Bistrot de Venise to learn the recipe. They make a wonderful coulis from the uva fragola grape, which is sweet and aromatic. Since these are almost impossible to get hold of outside Veneto we have used cherries instead. I particularly like using the macerated cherries from the Cherries in Wine recipe on page 249, but if you don't have them use fresh instead. The *frittelle* are also just as good on their own.

METHOD

Make the filling by blending the biscuits and sponges in a food processor into fine breadcrumbs. You can also do this by hand by putting them in a large, clean plastic bag and crushing with a rolling pin. Pour the crumbs into a large bowl, add the cheeses, almonds, egg yolks and sugar and combine to resemble a stiff paste. Use 2 dessertspoons to make quenelles (three-sided ovals) and lay these onto a baking tray lined with baking parchment. Place the tray into the freezer for around 3 hours or overnight to freeze solid.

To prepare the coulis, poach the cherries with the sugar in the wine in a medium saucepan, covered with a circle of baking parchment, for around 25 minutes or until soft. Remove from the heat, leave to cool and stone them. Purée with a hand-held blender or a food processor and rub through a sieve to make it really smooth.

To make the *frittelle*, heat the oil in a large high-sided frying pan to 175°C (345°F) until a drop of batter sizzles when it hits the oil. Put the flour and salt into a large mixing bowl and slowly whisk in the water until smooth. If any lumps remain, pour through a sieve. Put a few frozen quenelles at a time into the batter to coat and then use tongs to lift them out and gently drop into the hot oil. Take care not to splash yourself with oil or wear oven gloves to protect you. Deep-fry in batches for 2–3 minutes until golden brown. Remove with a slotted spoon and drain on paper towels. Serve immediately with the coulis at room temperature.

FOR THE FILLING

60 g (2 oz) amaretti biscuits

200 g (7 oz) trifle sponges

200 g (7 oz/scant 1 cup) mascarpone

200 g 7 oz/scant 1 cup) ricotta

100 g (3½ oz/1 cup) ground almonds

70 g (2½ oz) egg yolk (around 5 eggs (reserve the whites for meringues, see page 241)

60 g (2 oz/⅓ cup) icing (powdered) sugar

FOR THE CHERRY COULIS

500 g (1 lb 2 oz) cherries, macerated from the Cherries in Wine recipe (see page 249) or fresh

150 ml (5 fl oz/ ⅓ cup) Cherry Wine (see page 249) or white wine

100 g (3½ oz/scant ½ cup) caster (superfine) sugar

FOR THE BATTER

300 g (10½ oz/ 2½ cups) '00' plain (all-purpose) flour

Pinch of salt

500 ml (17 fl oz/ generous 2 cups) sparkling water

Sunflower oil for deep-frying

FRITTELLE ALLO ZABAIONE

Doughnuts filled with Zabaione Cream

MAKES 20-25

'I've just eaten five, God they're good,' was the message I received from Stefano Borella, our patisserie chef who we sent to Venice to cook in one of the best patisseries there, Rosa Salva in Calle Fiubera. It was here many years ago I ate four *frittelle*, stuffed to the brim with zabaglione cream, in one go, and I have been harping on about them ever since. After many attempts to recreate them back home we finally decided to send Stefano out to Venice to learn from the masters. This is their recipe. *Frittelle* are filled fried soft doughnuts and are traditionally made at *carnevale* time. Such is the demand that they are now made most of the year. The best *frittelle* have plenty of marsala, a sweet wine, in the cream and are well... soggy – but in the best possible way: they are soft and moist. Apparently this is due to the humidity in Venice, which makes the dough wet. One is simply not enough, as Stefano and I found out.

225 ml (8 fl oz/scant 1 cup) water

35 g (1¼ oz/generous 2 tbsp) unsalted butter

15 g (½ oz/1 tbsp) caster (superfine) sugar, plus extra to serve

7 g (¼ oz/1 heaped 1 tsp) salt

175 g (6 oz/1½ cups) '00' plain (all-purpose) flour

250 g (9 oz) eggs (around 4 large eggs), beaten

50 ml (2 fl oz/¼ cup) milk

50 g (1¾ oz/½ cup) sultanas (golden raisins) (optional)

2 drops of vanilla extract

2 litres (64 fl oz/8¼ cups) sunflower oil for deep-frying

METHOD

The pastry for the *frittelle* is made like choux pastry. Put the water, butter, sugar and salt into a saucepan over a medium heat to melt the butter. Pour in the flour in one go. Beat the mixture hard with a wooden spoon until the flour is well incorporated. Remove from the heat. Use a hand or electric whisk to beat in the eggs, a little at a time, until you have a smooth glossy mixture. Add the milk, sultanas and vanilla extract.

Heat the oil in a large high-sided frying pan or a deep-fat fryer to around 175°C (345°F) or until a small piece of bread sizzles as soon as it hits the fat. Take a heaped dessertspoonful of the mixture, pressing it against the side of the bowl as you remove it to get a quenelle, and use another spoon to gently push it off into the hot oil. Don't let it splash. Fry until dark golden brown, around 5 minutes, pushing them down gently with a slotted spoon. They will roll and turn themselves over which is great to watch. Remove with the slotted spoon and drain on paper towels to cool. Fill with the Zabaione Cream (half the quantity from the recipe opposite) or Vanilla Custard (half the recipe on page 232). Scatter with more caster sugar and serve. They are fine to freeze unfilled and can be kept in the refrigerator overnight, filled or unfilled.

CREMA ALLO ZABAIONE

Zabaione Cream

MAKES ENOUGH FOR THE *FRITTELLE*
OR 8 SERVINGS ON ITS OWN

This heavenly custard is what separates these doughnuts from any others. It is also wonderful poured over poached fruit or served in a cup with amaretti or baicoli biscuits for dunking.

500 ml (17 fl oz/
generous 2 cups)
milk

8 egg yolks

100 g (3½ oz/scant
½ cup) caster
(superfine)sugar,
plus 100 g (3½ oz/
scant ½ cup)
for dusting

100 g (3½ oz/scant
1 cup) strong white
(bread) flour

250 ml (8½ fl oz/
1 cup) Marsala,
warmed

150 ml (5 fl oz/
⅔ cup) whipping
cream

METHOD

Heat the milk over a medium heat in a large saucepan, but don't let it boil. In a mixing bowl, beat the egg yolks, sugar and flour together until smooth. Pour a ladleful of warm milk into the bowl and whisk through. Pour the egg mixture into the saucepan, stirring continuously, and heat until thickened. Add the warmed Marsala, whisking it in little by little. Transfer to a clean large bowl, cover with cling film (plastic wrap) and gently push the plastic wrap down so it is touching the surface of the custard. This is to stop a skin from forming. Set aside to cool. Whip the cream to soft peaks and, when the custard is cool, fold it into the cream.

Serve as it is or to fill the *frittelle*, scoop the cream into a piping bag with a nozzle. Use this to poke a hole in the *frittelle* and pipe in the custard. Dust with caster sugar and serve.

CIOCCOLATO CALDO

Hot Chocolate

SERVES 2

'"You're a rascal," I said. "Get two cups of chocolate ready directly after I have had my bath."' This quote is taken from Casanova's memoirs; apparently he was rather fond of hot chocolate. One of his favourite pastimes, other than the one he became famous for, was sipping hot chocolate in Florian's café on St Mark's Square. He would dip biscuits into sweet wine and hot chocolate. Nothing has really changed; Florian's are still serving rich, thick hot chocolate today in beautiful china cups as you can see in the photograph opposite.

METHOD

Put 30 g (1 oz/¼ cup) good-quality cocoa powder into a small bowl with 1 tablespoon of cornflour (cornstarch) and mix with 6 tablespoons of milk. Heat 250 ml (8½ oz/1 cup) milk in a saucepan and when hot – do not let the milk boil – stir in the cocoa mixture with 2 tablespoons of sugar. Whisk through and add 1 tablespoon of rum if you like at the end. Pour into warm coffee cups and serve with biscuits.

CREMA PASTICCERA

Vanilla Custard

MAKES ENOUGH FOR THE *FRITTELLE* OR 6 SERVINGS ON ITS OWN

This is a useful custard for serving with fruit pies such as the Venetian Pear Tart (see page 246), the Figs in Madeira (see page 253) or for filling *frittelle* (see page 228). To fill the *frittelle*, scoop the custard into a piping bag with a nozzle. Use this to poke a hole in the *frittelle* and pipe in the custard. Dust with caster sugar and serve.

METHOD

Heat the milk with the vanilla seeds in a large saucepan over a medium heat – don't let it boil. Whisk together the egg yolks, lemon zest, sugar and flour in a bowl. Add a ladleful of warm milk into the bowl and whisk this through. Pour the egg mixture into the saucepan with the rest of the milk. Stir with a wooden spoon until the mixture thickens, then remove from the heat. Transfer to a clean bowl and set aside to cool covered in cling film (plastic wrap) touching the surface of the custard. Whip the cream to soft peaks and fold into the cooled custard.

Keep covered in the refrigerator for up to 2 days.

500 ml (17 fl oz/ generous 2 cups) milk

Seeds from 1 vanilla pod (vanilla bean) or few drops of vanilla extract

2 egg yolks

Finely grated zest of 1 lemon

75 g (2½ oz/scant ⅓ cup) caster (superfine) sugar

100 g (3½ oz/scant ½ cup) strong white (bread) flour

Pinch of salt

150 ml (5 fl oz/ ⅔ cup) whipping cream

ZAETI VENEZIANI

Venetian Yellow Polenta Biscuits

MAKES 18-20

The word *zaeti* is Venetian dialect for *gialli*, meaning yellow. The colour comes from the polenta used to make them, which also gives them a wonderful crunch. They are made all over Venice, sometimes containing sultanas (golden raisins), orange or lemon zest. This recipe is from Rosa Salva patisserie.

METHOD

Preheat the oven to 180°C (350°F/Gas 4). Mix together all the ingredients in a food mixer or by hand. Depending on the size of your eggs, if you find the mixture very dry, add a couple of teaspoons of milk, or conversely add a little more polenta if the dough is very sticky. Take a handful of the dough and roll it into a sausage measuring around 2.5 cm (1 in) wide. Cut into 9 cm (3¾ in) lengths and roll each one gently to taper into a slightly pointed shape at each end. Lay onto a baking tray lined with baking parchment. Repeat this for all the dough. Bake for around 15–17 minutes until golden. Remove from the oven and cool on a wire rack. The biscuits will keep well in an airtight container for up to 1 week.

100 g (3½ oz/ scant ½ cup) salted butter

50 g (1¾ oz/¼ cup) caster (superfine) sugar

2 egg yolks

80 g (3 oz/⅓ cup) fine polenta

1 tsp baking powder

50 g (1¾ oz/½ cup) sultanas (golden raisins) (optional)

175 g (6 oz/1½ cups) '00' or plain (all-purpose) flour

1 tsp vanilla extract

4 tsp rum

Finely grated zest of 1 small orange

ESSE BURANEI

'S' *Biscuits* *from Burano*

MAKES 18–20

'These are the biscuits that I long to eat, soaked in wine, to fortify the stomach… composed of a little flour, an egg yolk, and a lot of sugar.' So Casanova wrote in his memoirs. These biscuits have been made on Casanova's native island of Burano for centuries and are featured in a 16th century fresco in the Villa Caldogno. They are also made in a ring shape, which was originally so that they could be stored on a rope aboard a ship. They are cooked to a crisp so that they last for weeks at sea. This recipe is from Rosa Salva patisserie. Originally they were made with lard, which gives a better, snappier result.

METHOD

Preheat the oven to 180°C (350°F/ Gas 4). Mix all the ingredients together in a food processor or by hand. Take a piece of the dough and roll into a long sausage shape 2 cm (¾ in) wide and cut into 10 cm (4 in) lengths. Shape the sausage into an 'S' shape and place on a baking tray lined with baking parchment. Repeat this for all the dough. Bake for 12–14 minutes until they are crisp and golden. Remove and cool on a wire rack.

200 g (7 oz/2 cups) '00' or plain (all-purpose) flour

100 g (3 ½ oz/ ⅓ cup) caster (superfine) sugar

75 g (2½ oz/ generous ¼ cup) lard or butter

1 egg

½ tsp vanilla extract

Finely grated zest of ½ lemon

MERINGHE

Basic Meringue

**MAKES 40–45 MERINGUES OR ENOUGH FOR THE MERINGUE
SEMIFREDDO WITH CHERRY COULIS (SEE PAGE 242)**

Meringues are popular in Venice; you see them everywhere, from delicate pink and pale green ones, white ones sandwiched together with chocolate and cream, to enormous puddings made from sponge cake and clouds of toasted meringue looking like a mother-in-law's hat at a wedding. There are various methods of making meringue but we find this is the best. It follows the Swiss method and is more robust than others when making flavoured meringues or using in a semifreddo.

METHOD

Put the egg whites and three-quarters of the sugar into a heatproof mixing bowl. Place the bowl over a pan of boiling water, making sure that the water does not touch the bowl. Whisk the egg mixture using an electric beater to 45°C (110°F) on a thermometer or until it becomes really thick and glossy. Carefully remove the bowl from the heat and stand it on a tea towel (dish cloth) so that the bottom dries and doesn't drip into the next bowl. Pour the mixture into a food mixer with a whisk attachment or use an electric beater and whisk until it doubles in size. Keep the whisk running and add the remaining sugar little by little.

Preheat the oven to 110°C (225°F/ Gas ¼). Flavour the meringues by folding in one of the flavours opposite or you can leave them plain. For the strawberry meringues, it is pretty to ripple the coulis (see how to make below) through the meringues rather than mix it all in. Pipe or spoon the meringue mixture onto baking trays lined with baking parchment, making them 4 cm (1¾ in) wide and 2–3 cm (¾–1¼ in) high.

Bake for around 30–40 minutes or until they are light to the touch, lift off easily, crisp on the outside and slightly soft of the inside. If you like them brittle, leave them in the oven for another 15 minutes.

FOR THE STRAWBERRY FILLING

Put the strawberries and sugar into a microwavable bowl and soften in the microwave for around 3–4 minutes or put into a small saucepan over a medium heat. When the strawberries can be squashed easily with a spoon against the side of the bowl or pan, they are done. Sieve the mixture to get rid of any large pips and allow to cool. The same can be done with raspberries.

125 g (4½ oz) egg whites (around

4 medium egg whites)

250 g (9 oz/ generous 1 cup) caster (superfine) sugar

FLAVOURINGS

PISTACHIO

50 g (1¾ oz/⅓ cup) pistachios, finely ground in a food processor

HAZELNUT

50 g (1¾ oz/ ⅓ cup) hazelnuts, toasted and finely ground in a food processor

STRAWBERRY

100 g (3½ oz/⅓ cup) strawberries

30 g (1 oz/2 tbsp) caster (superfine) sugar

SEMIFREDDO DI MERINGA CON SALSA ALLE CILIEGE

Meringue Semifreddo with Cherry Coulis

SERVES 6–8

This stunning dessert always delivers the wow factor. It is brilliant for entertaining as it can be left in the freezer until you need it and dressed with the fruit coulis at the last minute. We ate it at L'Osteria di Santa Marina and begged chef Agostino to give us the recipe. You can let your imagination run riot, adding fruit according to the season, nuts or even hot chocolate sauce.

METHOD

Preheat the oven to 120°C (250°F/ Gas ½). Line 3 baking sheets with baking parchment measuring at least 30 cm (12 in) square. Divide the meringue mixture into 3 and spread one third onto each sheet, making a circle or square around 1 cm (½ in) thick and 23 cm (9 in) across. This can be done using a cake tin as a mould and pushing the meringue flat with a spatula. Alternatively, draw a circle or square and use a piping bag to pipe a spiral of meringue to form the shape. Bake for 30–40 minutes or until crisp on the outside and slightly soft inside. Remove from the oven and allow to cool.

Put the cream, vanilla and icing sugar into a large bowl and whisk together to soft peaks. Place one of the meringues onto a plate and spread half the cream mixture on top. Put the second meringue on top and spread this with the rest of the cream. Top with the final meringue and freeze overnight. Remove from the freezer and cut into squares or circles by using a hot knife or pushing a ring mould into it. Either re-freeze at this point or serve straight away. If you re-freeze to use later, then take them out of the freezer 15 minutes before you wish to serve them. Serve with the Cherry Coulis and a glass of Cherry Wine (see page 249).

1 quantity of Basic Meringue (see page 241)

350 ml (12 fl oz/ 1⅓ cups) whipping cream

Seeds of 1 vanilla pod (vanilla bean) or 1 tsp vanilla extract

75 g (2½ oz/ generous ½ cup) icing (powdered) sugar

1 quantity of Cherry Coulis (see page 226)

BUDINO DI RISO AL LATTE DI MANDORLE

Almond Milk Rice Pudding with Cardamom and Orange

SERVES 8

In a beautiful, old hand-bound Venetian cookbook from the 1700s, we read the recipe for *Riso al latte di mandorle*, rice with almond milk sweetened with honey. The idea for it was probably brought to Venice by travellers from the Middle East. Nowadays it is made with cow's milk and given to children or the ill to fortify them. I love this way of cooking the rice first with butter and sugar, it creates a butterscotch flavour to this luscious creamy pudding.

METHOD

Melt the butter in a large saucepan over a medium heat. Mix the sugar and rice together in a bowl and then add to the butter, stirring for around 5 minutes so the rice is well coated in the butter and sugar. Add the milk and cream to the pan, then add the salt, cardamom, cinnamon and orange zest, and stir through to combine. Cook for around 25 minutes or until you have a thick, smooth rice pudding. Discard the flavourings. Serve at room temperature or cool and chill before serving. It will thicken on cooling, so add a dash of cream or milk to loosen it. Serve in glasses as it is or decorate with pistachios and a swirl of honey.

50 g (1¾ oz/ ½ stick) unsalted butter

35 g (1¼ oz/scant ¼ cup) caster (superfine) sugar

150 g (5½ oz) arborio rice

750 ml (25 fl oz/ 3 cups) homemade sieved Almond Milk (see page 222) or shop-bought unsweetened almond milk

450 ml (15 fl oz/ 2 cups) double (heavy) cream

Pinch of salt

3 cardamom pods

1 cinnamon stick

1 strip of orange zest, about 5 cm (2 in) long

30 g (1 oz/3 tbsp) shelled pistachios, roughly chopped (optional)

2 tbsp clear honey (optional)

TORTA DI PERE ALLA VENEZIANA

Venetian Pear Tart

SERVES 8 (MAKES 1 TART)

This wonderfully easy tart recipe is from our friend Monica Cesarato. She lives in Chioggia near to Venice and loves to use her local pears. At the shop near her house there were no less than five types available. The cinnamon in the pastry makes a delicious partner to the sweet pears. I like to serve it with the vanilla flavour Rich Custard Ice Cream Base on page 254 or the Whipped Mascarpone and Honey Cream (see page 248).

METHOD

To make the pastry, sift the flour into a large bowl and rub the butter into it using your fingertips until the mixture looks like fine breadcrumbs. Add the sugar, egg, cinnamon and salt. Mix well until you have a ball of dough. This can be done in a food processor. Cover the dough in cling film (plastic wrap) and put in the refrigerator for 30 minutes or overnight.

Preheat the oven to 200°C (400°F/Gas 6) and butter and lightly flour a 25 cm (10 in) loose-bottomed tart tin. After 30 minutes (if you chilled your pastry for longer, let it warm up a little for 20 minutes at room temperature) remove the pastry from the refrigerator, divide it in half and roll out into 2 circles. Line the tin with one of the circles of pastry.

Layer the sliced pears into the pastry case, sprinkle over the rum, if using, and top the pie with the second circle of pastry. Using a fork make some holes in the pastry to let the steam escape. Bake for around 25–30 minutes or until the pastry is golden.

FOR THE PASTRY

300 g (10½ oz/ 2½ cups) '00' or plain (all-purpose) flour

160 g (5¾ oz/ scant ¾ cup) unsalted butter

160 g (5¾ oz/scant ¾ cup) caster (superfine) sugar

1 egg

2 tsp ground cinnamon

Pinch of salt

FOR THE FILLING

5 large ripe pears, peeled and sliced

2 tbsp rum (optional)

CREMA DI MASCARPONE E MIELE

Whipped Mascarpone and Honey Cream

SERVES 10–12

Apparently Casanova enjoyed eating large amounts of mascarpone cheese and liked to share it with his lovers. Serve it in heaped dessertspoons with the Venetian Pear Tart (see page 246), macerated cherries from making the Cherries in Wine (opposite), Figs in Madeira (see page 253) or almost any dessert you can imagine!

METHOD

Put all the ingredients into a bowl and whisk together. Taste and adjust honey or rum as you like.

150 g (5½ oz/ ⅔ cup) mascarpone

100 ml (3½ fl oz/ scant ½ cup) double (heavy) cream

3 tbsp mild clear honey

1 tsp vanilla extract or seeds from 1 vanilla pod (vanilla bean)

1 tbsp rum or cognac or Grand Marnier

CILIEGIE MARINATE AL VINO

Cherries in Wine

SERVES 6–8 (MAKES 500 G/1 LB 2 OZ) MACERATED CHERRIES
AND 600 ML (20 FL OZ/2½ CUPS) CHERRY WINE

This is an idea inspired by the 14th century chef the Anonimo Veniziana. In the medieval days it was common for wealthy families to drink wine sweetened with ginger, honey and fruit before a meal as they believed it would open up their appetites. In Giancarlo's childhood his mother would preserve cherries from the summer harvest in wine or grappa to eat in winter. Drink the wine ice cold or warm. The cherries can be made into a coulis to serve with the Almond-filled Doughnuts (see page 226) or with Almond Ice Cream (see page 255).

METHOD

Put all the ingredients together into a medium saucepan and bring to the boil. Turn down the heat and simmer for 10 minutes. Taste and add more honey if necessary; if it is too sweet for you, add a little more wine. If the orange or cinnamon flavours are already strong enough for your taste, you can remove one or both at this point. The salt is there to give it a little more flavour and strangely it brings out the sweetness, so adjust it as you like but obviously you don't want it to taste salty. Remove from the heat and leave to cool. Store in the refrigerator for up to 2 weeks. If strained, the wine keeps for up to 1 month in the refrigerator.

To serve, either drain the cherries and serve them separately, make into a coulis or simply serve the mixture in tumblers or wine glasses.

500 g (1 lb 2 oz) cherries

4 cm (1½ in) piece fresh ginger, peeled and cut into 5 mm (¼ in) slices

3 cm (1¼ in) cinnamon stick

600 ml (20 fl oz/ 2½ cups) white or red wine

1 strip orange zest (use a potato peeler to peel the strip)

2 tbsp clear honey, to taste

Pinch of salt

CREMA FRITTA

Fried Custard

SERVES 4-6 (MAKES 16-18 DIAMONDS)

Warm, soft vanilla custard encased within a sugary crunchy coating. What more can I say? A delicacy during *carnevale* time in Venice, but so good all year round. Serve with hot chocolate or a fruit coulis to use for dunking.

METHOD

Line a 18 cm (7 in) 3 cm (1¼ in) baking tin with cling film (plastic wrap). Put the milk in a saucepan with the vanilla seeds or extract and orange or lemon zest and heat to just before it boils. Remove from the heat. Mix together the egg yolks, sugar and flour in a large bowl using a wooden spoon. Add the milk one ladleful at a time to the flour mixture, stirring constantly until half the milk is incorporated. Pour the mixture back into the rest of the milk in the saucepan. Return to the heat for around 5 minutes to thicken, stirring constantly. Remove from the heat and pour the custard into the lined tin. Cover the surface of the custard with plastic wrap so that the plastic wrap is touching the custard (this is to stop it forming a skin) and cool to room temperature.

Remove the plastic wrap and turn out the custard onto a work surface. Cut it into around 16–18 diamonds. Heat the sunflower oil in a large high-sided frying pan until around 175°C (345°F) or until a small piece of bread sizzles when it hits the oil. Dip the diamonds in the flour, then in egg, then in breadcrumbs to coat them all over. Deep-fry for around 10 minutes or until golden brown, turning halfway through the cooking time. Drain on paper towels and serve straight away.

500 ml (17 fl oz/
generous 2 cups)
milk

Seeds from
1 vanilla pod
(vanilla bean)
or 1 tsp vanilla
extract

Zest of 1 orange
or lemon, peeled
into lengths

5 egg yolks

80 g (2¾ oz) caster
(superfine) sugar

75 g (2½ oz) strong
white (bread)
flour, in a shallow
bowl, plus extra
for dusting

Sunflower oil
for deep-frying

1 egg, beaten, in
a shallow bowl

50 g (1¾ oz) fine
breadcrumbs, in
a shallow bowl

FICHI AL MADEIRA

Figs in Madeira

SERVES 4

Beautiful and simple, this has become my standby dessert recipe as long as I can find fresh figs. Something magical happens to figs when you cook them, especially when they take a warm bath of Madeira, a sweet wine from the islands of Madeira. Serve them warm with Vanilla or Almond Ice Cream (see pages 254 and 255).

METHOD

Preheat the oven to 180°C (350°F/Gas 4). Put the figs into a small, deep baking dish and pour over the Madeira and water. Cover with foil and bake in the oven for 45 minutes, removing the foil halfway through. Remove from the oven and allow to cool.

To make a syrup from the juices, pour them into a small saucepan and reduce over a medium heat until half of the original volume and slightly thickened. Serve at room temperature with Vanilla or Almond Ice Cream and the syrup poured over the top.

8 fresh figs

200 ml (7 fl oz/ scant 1 cup) Madeira

200 ml (7 fl oz/ scant 1 cup) water

GELATO ALLA CREMA

Rich Custard Ice Cream Base

MAKES 1.2 LITRES (40 FL OZ/5 CUPS)

This makes the kind of really smooth, heavenly ice cream served in Italian gelaterie. Once you have this mastered, you can add the flavourings below or have fun experimenting. You will need an ice cream maker.

METHOD

In a large saucepan, heat the milk and cream with half the sugar over a medium heat until just bubbling. Meanwhile, in a large bowl beat together the eggs and remaining sugar until smooth. Add 2 ladlefuls of hot milk to the egg mixture and immediately whisk together, then pour this back into the pan and whisk until thickened and will coat the back of the spoon.

To sterilise the ice cream, turn up the heat and increase the temperature of the mixture to 85°C (185°F), or until the ice cream coats the back of a spoon if you don't have a thermometer. Take off the heat immediately and pour into a bowl. To cool quickly, set this bowl over another full of iced water and then cover the surface of the custard with cling film (plastic wrap). Stir every so often. When the custard is at room temperature, churn in an ice-cream machine.

VANILLA

Add 1 teaspoon of vanilla extract or the seeds from one vanilla pod (vanilla bean) to the custard base in the bowl before mixing with the hot milk.

PANETTONE ICE CREAM

Blitz 150 g (5½ oz) panettone in a food processor until you have rough crumbs. We quite like pieces up to the size of a marble, so don't worry if it is not fine. Stir these crumbs into the cooling custard before churning in the machine.

CANDIED ORANGE ICE CREAM

Add 50 g (1¾ oz/¼ cup) finely chopped candied orange and the finely grated zest of one orange into the custard base in the bowl before stirring in the hot milk.

600 ml (20 fl oz/ 2½ cups) double (heavy) cream

400 ml (14 fl oz/ generous 1½ cups) whole milk

200 g (7 oz/scant 1 cup) caster (superfine) sugar

8 egg yolks

GELATO DI MANDORLE

Almond Ice Cream

SERVES 6–8

Almond milk was used a great deal in medieval Venice. I love the creamy texture and delicate nutty flavour. You can make your own following the recipe on page 222 or simply buy a good variety. I haven't made it too sweet but do add more sugar if you have a sweet tooth. If you want to leave out the dairy completely, substitute the cream for more almond milk but it will become more solid and icy rather than soft and creamy, so bring it out of the freezer 15 minutes before serving to allow it to soften.

METHOD

Heat around 100 ml (3½ fl oz/ scant ½ cup) of the milk in a saucepan over a medium heat and dissolve the sugar in it. When you can't feel any more granules of sugar, pour into a large bowl. Stir in the rest of the ingredients and leave to cool to room temperature. Churn in an ice-cream machine.

350 ml (12 fl oz/ 1⅓ cups) home-made Almond Milk (see page 222) or shop-bought

100 g (3½ oz/scant ½ cup) caster (superfine) sugar

350 ml (12 fl oz/1⅓ cups) double (heavy) cream

1 tbsp amaretto

30 g (1 oz) amaretti biscuits

GELATO AL LIMONE

Lemon Ice Cream

SERVES 4 (MAKES AROUND 650 ML/22 FL OZ/2¾ CUPS)

Delicious on its own and also for the Sgroppino drink below or serve with the Venetian Pear Tart on page 246.

METHOD

Dissolve the sugar into the milk with the lemon zest in a saucepan over a medium heat. Stir with a wooden spoon and as soon as you can't feel any granules of sugar left, remove from the heat and pour through a fine sieve into a bowl. Stir in the double cream and lemon juice. Allow to cool to room temperature, then churn in an ice-cream machine.

160 g (5¾ oz/scant ¾ cup) caster (superfine) sugar

250 ml (8 fl oz/ 1 cup) milk

Zest and juice of 2 lemons

250 ml (8 fl oz/ 1 cup) double (heavy) cream

SGROPPINO

Sgroppino

SERVES 4

This unusual drink/ice cream/cocktail combination is just heavenly. It's creamy, citrus-flavoured and sweet without being heavy. According to historian Francesco da Mosto, *sgroppino* comes from the word *desgropante*, which means 'something that unties knots' and therefore the drink aids digestion. Whatever the excuse for drinking it, kick off your heels at the end of a meal and enjoy!

METHOD

Put the ingredients into a blender or smoothie maker and whizz briefly until frothy and smooth. Pour into large chilled wine glasses.

1 quantity of Lemon Ice Cream (above) or 8 scoops of shop-bought ice cream

4 tbsp vodka

200 ml (7 fl oz/ scant 1 cup) Prosecco

Gianduja Semifreddo with Whipped Cream

SERVES 8–10

Venice's premier ice cream parlour is Gelateria Nico on the canal front opposite Giudecca island. They have become famous for the block of hazelnut and chocolate ice cream that they serve with whipped cream. In the restaurant Carampane they have paid homage to this stalwart of the Venetian gelaterie and serve a similar dessert. My goodness, it's good.

400 g (14 oz/ 1¾ cups) dark (bittersweet) chocolate with hazelnuts (filberts)

400 ml (14 fl oz/ generous 1½ cups) whipping cream

TO SERVE

Whipping cream, whipped to soft peaks

Caramel Hazelnuts (below)

METHOD

Line a 24 × 12 × 6 cm (9½ × 5 × 2½ in) loaf tin with cling film (plastic wrap). Put the chocolate into a food processor and blitz until it has a sand-like consistency; don't worry about a few lumps, a bit of texture is good. Fill a saucepan one-third full with hot water and put over a medium heat. Melt the chocolate in a heatproof bowl over the hot water, making sure the bottom of the bowl doesn't touch the water. Remove from the heat. In a separate bowl, whip the cream to soft peaks. Fold one-third of the cream into the warm chocolate. When it is well-blended, fold in the rest. Pour into the tin and transfer to the freezer to set overnight.

To serve, cut a slice of the semifreddo and put it into a glass, and add 2 tablespoons of whipped cream. Sprinkle over the broken caramel nuts and serve.

Caramel Hazelnuts

METHOD

Preheat the oven to 180°C (350°F/ Gas 4). Toast the hazelnuts in the oven on a baking tray for around 6–8 minutes until golden brown. Remove from the oven and set aside. Heat the sugar in a medium saucepan until it is caramel brown, add the nuts and stir through. Pour the mixture onto baking parchment on a baking tray and allow it to cool and set. Break up the nutty caramel into pieces with a rolling pin and scatter over ice cream.

100 g (3½ oz/scant ½ cup) caster (superfine) sugar

100 g (3½ oz/ ¾ cup) hazelnuts (filberts)

UVA SOTTO GRAPPA

Grapes Under Grappa

Cesare Benelli owns the fabulous Al Covo restaurant. He has been welcoming Venetians and visitors alike for years. Cesare's grandmother, Nonna Gina, used to make this in August and the jar of grapes would be opened at Christmas. In Italy the grape brings good luck, so it was thought to be a good luck charm for the forthcoming year. You will only find the uva sotto grappa at the restaurant in January and February and it is always given for free at the end of the meal. This is Nonna Gina's recipe.

METHOD

Thoroughly clean a large hermetically sealed jar. Use a bunch of the big moscato grapes, organic if possible, and clean them by wiping with a damp cloth rather than by rinsing under the tap, as we don't want the grapes to get too wet. Cut the grapes from the bunch leaving a tiny part of the stem attached to each grape. Weigh the grapes and note it down, then put the grapes into the jar. Work out 15% of the weight of the grapes (multiply the weight by 0.15) and add this amount of Acacia honey to the jar. Use quality white grappa to cover grapes completely. Seal the jar. Cover the jar completely in kitchen foil to block out any light and place it in a dark cupboard. Leave for at least 4–5 months – the longer, the better! Serve in little glasses at the end of a meal.

Katie and Giancarlo's Favourite Restaurants in Venice

AL COVO, CAMPIELLO DELLA PESCARIA, CASTELLO
WWW.RISTORANTEALCOVO.COM

Very good food. Owner Cesare is passionate about his choice of ingredients. Do book. They have a tiny, more modern sister restaurant called Il Covino down the road.

BAR ALL'ARCO
TEL: 041 520 5666

We love it here, it's always busy and the cicchetti are always fresh.

BISTROT DE VENISE, SAN MARCO, CALLE DEI FABBRI, VENEZIA
WWW.BISTROTDEVENISE.COM

Really great traditional food but also amazing historical food recreated from the work of Renaissance cooks. Do book and have the historical menu if you can, you won't taste anything as lovely and unusual as this elsewhere. The owner Sergio Fragiacomo is a passionate foodie, send him our regards.

CANTINA DO MORI, CALLE DO MORI
TEL: 041 522 5401

Do Mori dates back to 1462, making it the most ancient *bacaro* in Venice (even Casanova went there). It's full of character and history.

ENOITECA MASCARETA, CASTELLO, CALLE LUNGA SANTA MARIA FORMOSA
TEL: 041 523 0744

A buzzing place open late, go for a huge variety of wines, cheeses, quality antipasti plates as well as cooked food. Lovely atmosphere.

HARRY'S BAR, CALLE VALLARESSO
WWW.CIPRIANI.COM/US/HARRYS-BAR

Treat yourself to a Bellini or two and plate of carpaccio in their place of origin. It will always have a buzz about this place, there is nowhere else like it in the world. Eighty-year-old Arrigo still regularly frequents the bar keeping an eye on the food and service.

LA CANTINA, STRADA NUOVA, CANNAREGIO
TEL: 041 522 8258

Don't expect to rush Francesco Zorzetto as he meticulously prepares the food for you but it is amazing and worth the wait. Go for *cicchetti* or lunch or dinner. Watch his knife skills for the sheer joy of seeing an expert at work. And do try his selection of wonderful cheeses and artisan beers.

LOCANDA CIPRIANI, PIAZZA SANTA FOSCA, TORCELLO
WWW.LOCANDACIPRIANI.COM

We didn't manage a visit here but from all our reports it is well worth the journey to Torcello.

L'OSTERIA DI SANTA MARINA, CAMPO SANTA MARINA
TEL: 041 528 5239

Run by Danilo and his partner Agostino. It is elegant, food and service is outstanding. Agostino's food is traditional with a twist. It is best to book, especially in the evenings.

OSTERIA ALLE TESTIERE, CALLE DEL MONDO NOVO, CASTELLO
TEL: 041 522 7220

Tiny but busy place with great food, so you need to book well in advance.

TAVERNA LA FENICE, SAN MARCO
TEL: 041 522 3856

Just near the Fenice opera house. What a warm, comfortable and elegant place to eat. The wood panelling and warm lighting draws you in. We loved it. You have to try the potato *spuma on secoe* on a traditional Venetian stew served in a martini glass.

TRATTORIA ANTICHE CARAMPANE, SAN POLO
TEL: 041 524 0165
WWW.ANTICHECARAMPANE.COM

Tucked away next to the Ponte delle Tette in a less busy area behind the Rialto bridge. Really traditional but 'cool' feel and warm hospitality. Food is delicious, try a Gianduja semifreddo and a *Sgroppino* after dinner.

TRATTORIA DALLA MARISA, CANNAREGIO, FONDAMENTA DI SAN GIOBBE
TEL: 041 720 211

Great food cooked by chef Marisa for the locals at a good price. Do book and don't expect a choice.

TRATTORIA LA MADONNA, CALLE DELLA MADONNA, SAN POLO
WWW.RISTORANTEALLAMADONNA.COM

Near Rialto bridge and all the locals know it. Big and bustling, the waiters wear white tuxedos and work a long day including cleaning the spider crabs in the morning. Have the seafood risotto and black cuttlefish. Don't wear white.

VINI DA GIGIO, SESTIERE CANNAREGIO,
WWW.VINIDAGIGIO.COM

Venetian wine bar and restaurant run by a brother and sister. Traditional food but updated by this young couple. He can't eat wheat so there are lots of alternatives for those like him. Try the borlotti bean and pasta soup – it makes you sigh with comfort. Wash it down with Prosecco in the style of the *contadino* (peasant farmer), cloudy and light but full of flavour and dry.

VINO VERO CANNAREGIO, FONDAMENTA DI MISERICORDIA,
TEL: 041 275 0044
WWW.VINOVERO.WINE

Very good bar with a big selection of biodynamic wines.

For the best patisserie visit

PASTICCERIA ROSA SALVA, CALLE FIUBERA WWW.ROSASALVA.IT

Try the *frittelle* stuffed with zabaglione cream.

PASTICCERIA RIZZARDINI, LOCALITA SAN POLO

PASTICCERIA TONOLO, LOCATED IN CALLE DE SAN PANTALON ARE ALSO GREAT.

On the pretty island of Burano

Go for lunch and have a walk around this colourful toy-town-like island; the two best places are:

IL GATTO NERO, FONDAMENTA DELLA GUIDECCA WWW.GATTONERO.COM

Run by father and son team. Massimo is the son and charms the visitors speaking English with a Scottish accent while dad works furiously in the kitchen making just delicious food. Sit outside and watch the world go by.

TRATTORIA DA ROMANO, VIA GALUPPI, BURANO WWW.DAROMANO.IT

The oldest restaurant on the island, full of charm and run by the original family. Grandma and mum cook in the kitchen while dad serves the customers. They are busy and bustling and serve simple, traditional food. The *fritto misto* and risotto are their specialties, ask to watch Mirko throw the risotto in the pan.

On the glass-making island of Murano

BUSA ALLA TORRE DA LELE TEL: 041 739 662

You don't need an address, just ask when you get off the boat.

Flame-haired Viking-like Lele shops, cooks and breathes Venetian food. Very traditional and good cooking from a passionate man.

AL MERCÀ, SAN POLO

As its name suggests, it is near the old market at Rialto and sells really good *cicchetti*. You have to stand outside as the bar is minuscule. Go at 6pm and mix with the locals drinking Spritz and eating meatballs.

Bacari – bars that sell *cicchetti* and drinks

These are great, often stand-up, bars where the locals go for a snack like little fried meatballs or tiny filled panini. You can sit down in some but they are often small. Drink Prosecco or order an Aperol or Campari Spritz. No need to book unless you want to sit down. There are so many bars but these are our favourites.

CANTINA DO SPADE, SAN POLO TEL: 041 521 0583

Serves risotto to the locals at 12 noon, *cicchetti* and simple plates, good for lunch or light supper. It's snug, warm and busy, so good on a cold day.

IL CANTINONE GIÀ SCHIAVI, FONDAMENTA NANI, IN THE DORSODORO AREA

A really lovely wine shop, bar and café all in one serving *cicchetti* made by the owner Allesandra de Respinis. She has written a book about her recipes which you can buy. Lovely atmosphere and choice.

Things to do

ROW VENICE HTTPS://ROWVENICE.ORG

Take a rowing lesson with Row Venice or better still a Cicchetti Row when you are shown how to row a gondola and you stop off at bars along the way! Our guide was Nan and she is really knowledgeable about wines as well as rowing.

WWW.COOKINVENICE.COM

Take an authentic and informative cooking lesson with two fun local ladies; Monica and Arianna, or let Monica take you for a tour of her favourite *cicchetti* bars.

Places to stay

PALAZZETTO PISANI WWW.PALAZZETTOPISANI.COM

Or try: WWW.THECITYAPARTMENTBOOK.COM

The wonderful Palazzetto Pisani is where we stayed and shot much of the book.

KATIE CALDESI WWW.CALDESI.COM

FOR VENETIAN COOKING LESSONS IN THE UK, AND FOR INFORMATION ON OUR RESTAURANTS, VISIT: WWW.CALDESI.COM

FIRST ROW FROM LEFT TO RIGHT:

Luca Piazza,
Massimiliano
Bovo,
Monica Ceserato,
Francesco
Agopyan

SECOND ROW FROM LEFT TO RIGHT:

Rugero Bovo,
Chef Willy,
Ivan di Rossi and
his wife Ariana,
Arrigo Cipriani

THIRD ROW FROM LEFT TO RIGHT:

Luigi Seno,
Ada Catto,
Antonio Rosa
Salva, Danilo
Baldan

FOURTH ROW FROM LEFT TO RIGHT:

Paolo Lazzari,
Sergio
Fragiacomo,
Helen Cathcart,
Kate Pollard

Grazie,
Thank you

KATE POLLARD, PUBLISHER

Thank you for steering the ship with your graceful calm and for giving us the opportunity to write a book about this dreamy place, it has been an honour to write about it. We have fallen in love with Venice.

HELEN CATHCART, PHOTOGRAPHER

Your stunning photography always overwhelms us, as well as your boundless energy and sense of fun. Already looking forward to the next trip together.

SUSAN PEGG, EDITOR

We've never met but I feel as though we know one another. You have beautifully shaped, organised and trimmed without offence and I look forward to working with you much more.

KAJAL MISTRY, SENIOR EDITOR

Thanks for all your help.

SHEILA KEATING

Thank you for making sense of my initial scrawls, I love your honesty and for knowing what I really want to say.

SHEILA ABELMAN

Our literary agent, thank you for taking care of us.

WE WOULD LIKE TO SAY A BIG THANK YOU TO THE FOLLOWING PEOPLE, FOR THEIR GENEROSITY WITH THEIR TIME AND PATIENCE WITH MY ENDLESS QUESTIONS:

LUCA PIAZZA

Thank you for taking time out from being an architect to guide us at some pace through the back alleys of Venice so as to avoid slow moving tourists and bad restaurants.

SERGIO FRAGIACOMO AND MARIO

The chef at Bistrot de Venise for letting us into your fabulous restaurant. The historical research you have done and the resulting recipes have opened up a whole new world for us. The historical meal you gave us was one of the most memorable and superb meals of my life.

PATISSERIE ROSA SALVA

Thank you so much to Antonio Rosa Salva for letting Stefano come and work with you and allowing us to use your recipes. He learnt so much and loved being with your staff. Your fritelle allo zabaione are just fantastic!

L'OSTERIA DI SANTA MARINA

Thank you so much to Danilo and Agostino for your recipes and help.

ROGER AND SHEILA BROCKLEHURST

My wonderful godparents who, luckily for me, have a huge interest in history, Italy and food. Thank you for all your invaluable research and humour.

MONICA CESARATO

You are a star. You have been invaluable in our quest to find great Venetian cooking and thank you to you and Arianna for all of your lovely recipes.

IVAN AND HIS TEAM AT THE PASTIFICIO SERENISSIMA IN VENICE

Thank you for your time and inspired recipes.

WILLY THE CHEF

I learnt a lot from our chat together, thank you for spending time with us.

BRIAN MCLEOD

Thank you for doubling-checking my facts and giving your opinion at all times!

LOUISE SMITHSON

Thank you so much for your advice on historical cooking from the other side of the pond and for your careful and accurate online translation of the Anonimo Veneziano.

IAN BETHWAITE AND CARRIE DARBY

Our brilliant friends, researchers, recipe testers – thank you for always seeming delighted with Chicken and Ginger and pies over and over again while we perfected the recipes!

MANJULA SAMARASINGHE

Thank you for joining us on our journey into Venetian food, for your ideas, enthusiasm, help and knowledge of spices.

PALAZZETTO PISANI

Thank you for letting us shoot your beautiful place.

ARRIGO CIPRIANI

It was a real pleasure to meet you, to hear your story and that of Harry's Bar and Venice itself. Thank you so much for the recipes and your time.

RUSSELL NORMAN

Thank you for generously sharing your Venetian contacts and advising us where to go.

Bibliography

ACKROYD, PETER, *VENICE*, CHATTO & WINDUS, 2010

Fascinating and entertaining at the same time, Ackroyd brings the history to life, from the origins of Venice to the effect of the tourists of the present day.

AGOSTINI, PINO AND ALVISE, ZORZI, *VENICE: TRADITION AND FOOD*, ARSENALE EDITRICE, 2004

The history of Venetian food and traditional Venetian recipes.

ANONIMO VENEZIANO (ANONYMOUS VENETIAN), *LIBRO PER CUOCO (BOOK FOR COOK)*, 14TH CENTURY

The original, written by hand in brown ink is in the Biblioteca Casanatense in Rome. The online version in Italian can be found at www.staff.uni-giessen. de/gloning/tx/frati.htm in Venetian dialect. For the English translation by Louise Smithson look at her fascinating site on medieval cookery at http:// www.medievalcookery.com/helewyse/ libro.html. I loved to read Louise's translation, particularly having held and read the original, it saved me hours of translating from the Venetian dialect. The writer really did refer to his recipes as 'perfect' and 'quick'.

CASANOVA, GIACOMO, *THE STORY OF MY LIFE*, TRANSLATED BY STEPHEN SARTARELLI AND SOPHIE HAWKES, PENGUIN, 2001

Like or dislike him, I am glad he wrote in such detail about his life and the food he ate.

CIPRIANI, HARRY, *THE HARRY'S BAR COOKBOOK*, JOHN BLAKE, 2006

The history of Harry's Bar and its world famous recipes.

DA MOSTO, FRANCESCO, *FRANCESCO'S KITCHEN*, EBURY PRESS, 2007

A look at Venice and its food through the eyes of a Venetian, his personal favourites as well as the traditional dishes.

DA MOSTO, FRANCESCO, *FRANCESCO'S VENICE*, BBC BOOKS, 2004

Published as a tie-in to his television series, it is full of beautiful images that illustrate da Mosta's easy-to-read view of Venetian history.

DE RESPINIS, ALESSANDRA, *CICCHETTARIO*, PELLITIASSOCIATI

Allessandra's list of her favourite *cicchetti* and their ingredients.

DEL CONTE, ANNA, *THE CLASSIC FOOD OF NORTHERN ITALY*, PAVILION, 1999

A trustworthy and valuable source of Italy's great recipes.

EDWARDS, JOHN, *THE ROMAN COOKERY OF APICIUS*, RANDOM HOUSE, 1993

A translation of the Latin *De Re Coquinaria*, 'On Cookery' by Apicius from around late 4th to early 5th century AD.

GILMOUR, DAVID, *THE PURSUIT OF ITALY*, PENGUIN, 2012

An easily-readable book that we recommend to anyone wishing to learn more about the history of this amazing peninsula.

WWW.INMAMASKITCHEN

An American website full of facts and recipes from around the world.

KELLY, IAN, *CASANOVA: ACTOR, SPY, LOVER, PRIEST*, HODDER & STOUGHTON, 2008

It's a great read, and one that is well researched, following Casanova and his various adventures across Europe. In addition to his interest in the fairer sex, the book also brings out Casanova's love of food, with a chapter on Casanova's claim to be one of the earliest food writers. Actually this chapter is pretty short, but amongst the archive of his writings there are over 200 recipes that he collected during his lifetime.

MARTINO MAESTRO, *LIBRO DE ARTE COQUINARIA (THE ART OF COOKING)*, 1465

Martino was chef to the rich and powerful and wrote down his fascinating Renaissance recipes. Gillian Riley has translated it into English for Octavo in 2005.

ROBINSON, JANCIS, *THE OXFORD COMPANION TO WINE*, OXFORD COMPANIONS, 1994

An invaluable and authoritative reference book on the world of wine.

SALVATORI DE ZULIANI, MARIU, *A TOLA CON I NOSTRI VECI*, FRANCOANGELI, 2001

Around a thousand Venetian recipes collected and published so that they are never forgotten.

SCULLY, TERENCE (TRANSLATOR), THE OPERA OF BARTOLOMEO SCAPPI (1570): L'ARTE ET PRUDENZA D'UN MAESTRO CUOCO (THE ART AND CRAFT OF A MASTER COOK), LORENZO DA PONTE ITALIAN LIBRARY

Scappi was the most famous Renaissance chef and this volume brings to life how food was prepared and eaten during this incredible period of history.

SPECTOR, SALLY, *VENICE AND FOOD*, ARSENALE EDITRICE, 1998

A beautiful book full of stories, history, illustrations and recipes by Sally Spector. One to pore over in bed with a cup of cocoa.

STRATHERN, PAUL, *THE SPIRIT OF VENICE, FROM MARCO POLO TO CASANOVA*, PIMLICO 2013

I couldn't put this book down, if only my history teachers at school could have brought history to life in the way of Paul Strathern. So many fascinating stories I wanted to repeat them all. Buy this book.

WRIGHT, CLIFFORD A, *A MEDITERRANEAN FEAST: THE STORY OF THE BIRTH OF THE CELEBRATED CUISINES OF THE MEDITERRANEAN FROM THE MERCHANTS OF VENICE TO THE BARBARY CORSAIRS*, WILLIAM MORROW AND COMPANY, 1999

Over a thousand years of history and 500 recipes, an essential reference book for anyone interested in Mediterranean food.

Index

A

almonds
almond-filled doughnuts with cherry coulis 226-7
almond ice cream 255
almond milk 222
almond milk rice pudding with cardamom and orange 244-5

artichokes
artichoke and Parmesan pie 68-9
marinated artichokes 162-3

asiago cheese
turkey stuffed with asiago cheese and speck 218

asparagus
broad bean, asparagus and courgette salad 146-7

aubergines
aubergine balls 23
red peppers, aubergines and onions 159

B

bacon
bacon, chestnut and barley soup 124-5

beans 144-5

beef
little meat patties 22
raw beef salad 54
rich beef stew with Parmesan mash 210-11
salted beef 36-7

beetroot
half moons of pasta filled with beetroot in poppy seed butter 96-7

biscuits
's' biscuits from Burano 236-7
Venetian yellow polenta biscuits 234-5

borlotti beans and pasta soup 122

broad bean, asparagus and courgette salad 146-7

butter bean and mint salad 148

C

cabbage
smothered green cabbage 171

carrots
buttered carrots with herbs 167

cauliflower
spiced cauliflower or broccoli with raisins 164

cherries
almond-filled doughnuts with cherry coulis 226-7
cherries in wine 249
meringue semifreddo with cherry coulis 244-5

chicken
chicken with ginger, saffron and dates 220-1
cop's chicken risotto 136-7
fantastic chicken with fennel and fine spices 223
Rita's chicken stock 116
spicy fennel seed chicken 52

chocolate
Gianduja semifreddo with whipped cream 261
hot chocolate 230-1

clams
clams in ginger broth 182-3
razor clams with garlic and parsley 184-5

cod
creamy salt cod 181

crab
black linguine with crab 78-9

cream
Gianduja semifreddo with whipped cream 261
whipped mascarpone and honey cream 248
zabaione cream 229

crostini
ricotta and walnut crostini 32

custard
fried custard diamonds 250-1
rich custard ice cream base 254
vanilla custard 232

cuttlefish
black cuttlefish 201

D

doughnuts
almond-filled doughnuts with cherry coulis 2 26-7
doughnuts filled with zabaione cream 228-9

dressings 54
juniper dressing 188-9
raw fish salad with a citrus dressing 56-7

drinks 18-21
hot chocolate 230-1
sgroppino 259

duck breasts with peverada sauce and spiced apple compote 216-17

E

eel in bay leaves 190-1

eggs
basic frittata 154-5

F

figs in Madeira 252-3

fish
Ada's fish soup with saffron 126-7
batter for frying 53
deep-fried fish and vegetables 49
fish stock 117

frittata, basic 154-5

G

game
good game pie 65
pot roast game in wine 206-7

garlic sauce for meat 219

gnocchi
potato gnocchi 100-1
pumpkin gnocchi and lamb ragù 104
pumpkin stuffed gnocchi 102-3

gorgonzola
cocoa ravioli stuffed with gorgonzola and walnuts 92-3

grapes under grappa 262-3

Index

H

hazelnuts
  caramel hazelnuts 261
horseradish sauce 169

I

ice cream
  almond ice cream 255
  candied orange ice cream 254
  Gianduja semifreddo with whipped cream 261
  lemon ice cream 259
  panettone ice cream 254
  rich custard ice cream base 254
  sgroppino 259

K

kale
  black kale and apple 168
kippers
  smoked fish risotto 134–5

L

lamb ragù with spices 107
lemon ice cream 259
linguine
  black linguine with crab 78–9
  linguine with seafood 82–3
liver
  Venetian liver and onions 213

M

Madeira 20
  figs in Madeira 252–3
mascarpone
  whipped mascarpone and honey cream 248
meringues
  basic meringue 240–1
  meringue semifreddo with cherry coulis 244–5

milk, almond 222
mozzarella
  sun-dried tomato with mozzarella and basil 38–9
mushrooms
  porcini and pecorino strudel 70–1
  spelt spaghetti with wild mushrooms and Parmesan cream 76–7

O

onions
  sweet and sour onions 41
oranges
  candied orange ice cream 254

P

panettone ice cream 254
Parmesan
  cocoa tagliatelle with cheese sauce 91
patties
  aubergine balls 23
  little meat patties 22
  tuna patties 24–5
pears
  Venetian pear tart 246–7
peas
  rice and peas 139
pecorino
  cheese filled ravioli in saffron and herb sauce 94–5
peppers 156
  pepper risotto 133
  red peppers, aubergines and onions 159
  roasted red pepper sauce 156
  turbot with three pepper and juniper dressing 188–9
pesto 32–3
pies 63
  artichoke and Parmesan pie 68–9

fantastic cheese, spinach and leek pie 66–7
  good game pie 65
polenta 108–11
  black and white polenta squares 34–5
  black polenta 111
  Venetian yellow polenta biscuits 234–5
pomegranates
  perfect and quick pomegranate and ginger sauce 208–9
potatoes
  potato gnocchi 100–1
  rich beef stew with Parmesan mash 210–11
prawns
  crispy prawns on sweet and sour pumpkin 202–3
  prawn risotto 142
  spaghetti with prawns and tomato 80–1
pumpkin 176
  crispy prawns on sweet and sour pumpkin 202–3
  pumpkin gnocchi and lamb ragù 104
  pumpkin in saor 177
  pumpkin risotto 133
  pumpkin soup 118
  pumpkin stuffed gnocchi 102–3
  roast pumpkin puree 177

R

ravioli
  cheese filled ravioli in saffron and herb sauce 94–5
  cocoa ravioli stuffed with gorgonzola and walnuts 92–3
  Rita's ravioli 90
rice
  almond milk rice pudding with cardamom and orange 244–5
ricotta
  ricotta and walnut crostini 32

risottos

basic Venetian risotto method 129
black risotto 133
cop's chicken risotto 136–7
lemon and Prosecco risotto 133
pepper risotto 133
prawn risotto 142
pumpkin risotto 133
rice and peas 139
smoked fish risotto 134–5

rolls

little salted bread rolls 60–1
toasted bread & little filled rolls 30–1

S

salads

broad bean, asparagus and courgette salad 146–7
butter bean and mint salad 148
raw beef salad 54

salmon

raw fish salad with a citrus dressing 56–7

sandwiches 28–9

sardines

breadcrumbed sardines 50–1
golden fried sardines 50
pasta with sardines and onions 75
sweet and sour sardines with onions, pine nuts and raisins 42–3

sauces

duck breasts with peverada sauce and spiced apple compote 216–17
garlic sauce for meat 219
horseradish sauce 169
perfect and quick pomegranate and ginger sauce 208–9
roasted red pepper sauce 156
saffron and herb sauce 94–5

sea bass and clams on lamon beans 192–3

seafood

linguine with seafood 82–3
seafood on the grill 198–9
seafood stock 117

sole

pan-fried dover sole 196–7
sole and prawns in saor 46

soup

Ada's fish soup with saffron 126–7
bacon, chestnut and barley soup 124–5
borlotti beans and pasta soup 122
pumpkin soup 118

spaghetti

spaghetti with prawns and tomato 80–1
spelt spaghetti with wild mushrooms and Parmesan cream 76–7

stock

fish stock 117
Rita's chicken stock 116
seafood stock 117
vegetable stock 115

strudels

porcini and pecorino strudel 70–1

T

tomatoes

sun-dried tomato with mozzarella and basil 38–9

tuna patties 24–5

turbot with three pepper and juniper dressing 188–9

turkey stuffed with asiago cheese and speck 218

V

veal

Rita's ravioli 90

vegetables

fantastic cheese, spinach and leek pie 66–7
grilled vegetables 152–3
roasted root vegetables 172–3
vegetable stock 115

About the Authors

Owners of London's Caldesi in Marylebone, Caldesi in Campagna in Bray, and the Marylebone La Cucina Caldesi cooking school, Katie and Giancarlo Caldesi have a passion for Italian food. They have spent over 25 years teaching students at every level, and have written 17 cookbooks. Katie and Giancarlo have two children, Giorgio and Flavio.